DATE DUE

NOV 24 2011			

Demco

WEB LITERACY
for
EDUCATORS

WEB LITERACY *for* EDUCATORS

ALAN NOVEMBER

CORWIN PRESS
A SAGE Company
Thousand Oaks, CA 91320

For information:

Corwin Press
A SAGE Company
2455 Teller Road
Thousand Oaks, California 91320
www.corwinpress.com

SAGE Ltd.
1 Oliver's Yard
55 City Road
London EC1Y 1SP
United Kingdom

SAGE India Pvt. Ltd.
B 1/I 1 Mohan Cooperative
    Industrial Area
Mathura Road, New Delhi
India 110 044

SAGE Asia-Pacific Pte. Ltd.
33 Pekin Street #02-01
Far East Square
Singapore 048763

Printed in the United States of America.

Library of Congress Cataloging-in-Publication Data

November, Alan C.
 Web literacy for educators/Alan November.
    p. cm.
Includes bibliographical references and index.
ISBN 978-1-4129-5842-4 (cloth)
ISBN 978-1-4129-5843-1 (pbk.)
    1. Internet in education—United States. 2. Computer network resources—United States—Evaluation. 3. Critical thinking—United States. I. Title.

LB1044.87.N68 2008
371.33'44678—dc22   2007047566

This book is printed on acid-free paper.

08   09   10   11   12   10   9   8   7   6   5   4   3   2   1

Acquisitions Editor:	Hudson Perigo
Editorial Assistant:	Lesley Blake
Production Editor:	Jenn Reese
Copy Editor:	Trey Thoelcke
Typesetter:	C&M Digitals (P) Ltd.
Proofreader:	Victoria Reed-Castro
Indexer:	Nara Wood
Cover Designer:	Lisa Miller

Contents

Preface

But I read it on the Internet—it must be true!

The Internet is the most powerful, convenient, and potentially manipulative medium ever invented. It can give you any version of the truth you are looking for. Not only does information expand and change every day, the rules for finding information also change.

For many students, the Web is the dominant medium and the place they most likely go to find information. Unfortunately, many students accept information that looks authentic as the "truth" and this is one of the dangers of researching on the Web—especially since anyone can publish almost anything they want.

The ability to think critically about Web information is an essential skill for teachers and students. Web literacy goes beyond reading the content of a Web page (which is still an important step!). It also means becoming knowledgeable in the grammar of the Internet:

- Knowing how to read a URL
- Finding out who published a Web site
- Looking to see who is linked to a site

Being Web literate means you understand how search engines work and how information is controlled. It also means you have the skills to perform powerful searches that can potentially save time and frustration.

The purpose of this guidebook is to help teachers and students learn more about Web literacy and develop critical-thinking skills. It is a practical resource full of exercises, tips, handouts, and stories drawn from educators around the country. There is a wide variety of activities to use in the classroom or try on your own. You will be introduced to a multitude of skill sets and helpful resources.

BUILDING KNOWLEDGE CHAPTER BY CHAPTER

This book begins by explaining the basics of the Internet, setting the stage by introducing scaffolds and terminology critical to developing Web literacy skills. As chapters progress, so does the complexity of information. Depending on your level of comfort with the Web, you may wish to skip over various sections.

Chapter 1—Web Basics for Critical Thinking

- The Essentials
- Exploring the Grammar of the Internet

Chapter 2—The Empowered Researcher

- How Do Search Engines Work?
- Who Controls Information on the Internet?

Chapter 3—Get REAL: How to Validate Information on the Web

- Read the URL
- Examine the Content
- Ask About the Author and Owner

Chapter 4—Look at the Links

- Forward Links and Back Links

Chapter 5—Research Outside the Box: A Guide to Smart Searching

- Search With Extensions
- Creating a Virtual Index
- Finding Resources in Teacher Web Sites
- Calling All Colleagues

Chapter 6—Expanding the Boundaries: Blogs, RSS, Podcasts, and Wikis

- Blogs
- RSS
- Podcasts
- Wikis

Chapter 7—Strategies and Evaluation: Putting It All Together

- Get REAL
- REAL Resources

HOW TO USE THIS BOOK

This book is designed to provide hands-on activities that allow you to practice and explore new concepts as they are introduced. Some of these activities may be used with students—some are designed for you to try on your own. Look for these headings for clarification:

Try This—Under this heading you will find activities for teachers to do on their own or preview first before using in the classroom. Activities in these sections often focus on professional development issues, such as how to find teacher resources in specific Web sites or from other teachers around the world. They may contain examples that may not be appropriate for all ages of student audiences.

Student Review—This heading refers to information that is recommended to review with students prior to beginning a For Students activity. Student Reviews outline important questions or considerations central to the Web literacy concept being introduced.

For Students—This refers to activities to try in the classroom. Often there are sites provided for you, or in some instances you are encouraged to find your own, related to your particular subject area. Any worksheets used in a For Students activity will be found at the end of each chapter.

Assessment—At the end of each chapter, you will find a formative assessment to use with your students. These multiple choice questions review the skills and terminology introduced in each chapter. An answer key is included.

Questions for Further Thought and Discussion—These questions are to be used as you think more deeply about the content presented in this book. The questions are designed to spur discussion among your peers.

I hope you find this guide to be a practical and worthwhile investment of your valuable time.

On the Web

To supplement the material found in this book, we have created a Web page (http://www.novemberlearning.com/publications) that provides direct access to all of the links included within each chapter. This will make exploring the sites noted in the book much easier for you, and it will allow us to keep the links current should any of their addresses change.

Additionally, we are including all of the *Questions for Further Thought and Discussion* found at the end of each chapter on this same Web page. Over time, we will be adding more questions to this list to continually help you broaden the range of discussion within your school communities.

Should you find a Web address that needs to be changed, or if you would like to suggest thought-provoking questions that could be added to this list, we encourage you to e-mail this information to feedback@november learning.com. We also encourage you to use this same e-mail address to share stories of student experience. With your permission, your ideas may be included in future editions of *Web Literacy for Educators*.

Acknowledgments

More than any other book I have written, *Web Literacy for Educators* has had direct input from many creative voices. Christine Bridge, Brian Mull, Chris Turek, and Jim Wenzloff from the November Learning Team, have helped to research the stories and the technical descriptions of many of the web literacy tools. Inspiring work from classroom teachers such as Darren Kuropatwa from Winnipeg, Manitoba; Bob Sprankle of Wells, Maine; and Chris Burnett from Michigan have given depth to the power of applying Web literacy to help children of all backgrounds expand their boundaries of learning.

My own children, Danny and Jessie, continue to motivate and challenge me to stretch my understanding of the emerging culture of our youth who are so facile with the tools but who do need the guidance of their teachers to help integrate their digital world with our curriculum.

I am very grateful to all of my workshop participants who have challenged me to explain things in different ways and who have added to my own understanding of how to rethink my sense of the challenges we can give our children.

I am sure that I will be grateful to many of you who are willing to use this book as a resource and to share your stories and your questions at our Web site.

We are at a time when must expand the boundaries of learning. My hope is that *Web Literacy for Educators* will be a logical place to begin a journey that will lead to students who are more motivated and excited about learning and most importantly, who want to make a contribution to their class and to their communities.

Corwin Press gratefully acknowledges the contributions of the following individuals:

Cheryl Oakes
Collaborative Content Coach for Technology
Wells Ogunquit CSD
Wells, ME

Betsy Muller
Ed. Tech. Consultant and Technology Teacher
Issaquah School District
Seattle, WA

About the Author

 **Alan November** is an international leader in education technology. He began his career as an oceanography teacher and dorm counselor at an island reform school for boys in Boston Harbor. He has been director of an alternative high school, computer coordinator, technology consultant, and university lecturer. He has helped schools, governments, and industry leaders improve the quality of education through technology.

Alan's areas of expertise include planning across curriculum, staff development, new school design, community building, and leadership development. He has delivered keynotes and workshops in all 50 states, across Canada, and throughout the United Kingdom, Europe, Asia, and Central America.

Alan was named one of the nation's fifteen most influential thinkers of the decade by Classroom Computer Learning Magazine. In 2001, he was listed one of eight educators to provide leadership into the future by the Eisenhower National Clearinghouse. His writings include numerous articles and the best-selling book, *Empowering Students With Technology.* Alan was cofounder of the Stanford Institute for Educational Leadership through Technology and is most proud of being selected as one of the original five national Christa McAuliffe Educators.

Each summer Alan leads the Building Learning Communities summer conference with world-class presenters and participants from all over the world. Visit http://www.novemberlearning.com/blc/ for more details.

Introduction

Long, long ago, there was a magical invention called paper. Children learned quickly how to use this new technology for activities such as reading and writing, long before many of their teachers and parents knew how. It was so much faster, easier (and lighter!) than stone and chisel.

The children were excited about all of the possibilities of this new technology. They could express themselves to the world! However, since there were few adult role models to provide proper guidance, some children abused this newfound power. Middle school girls were known to write mean and nasty notes to one another. Boys were spending way too much time using it for playing games rather than accomplishing something worthwhile. Paper was causing all sorts of problems.

When the adults found out what the children were up to with the technology, they were horrified. Paper had to be stopped! It was making the children do bad things and they needed to be protected. And so it was decided that paper should be banned from schools. The children were not upset because they knew they could still use the new technology when they were outside of school. It was free and there was nothing to stop them from accessing all that they wanted without parents and teachers even knowing. Banning paper from the schools did not help curb the children's abuse of it. In fact, things became much, much worse.

Years later, some of the adults, particularly the educators, reconsidered the original ban and decided to embed the technology into the process of learning. Paper became the primary media of learning and entirely replaced stone and chisel. Adults provided role models every day for reading and producing content. A new literacy was born and children were taught how to apply it across the curriculum.

It turned out that paper made life much easier. You could create content and not have to move around heavy stone. Historians credit the new paper technology for the foundation of the Renaissance and the eventual development of democracy.

Centuries later, a new and even more powerful technology emerged that started to replace paper. It was called the Internet. Once again, many children started to use it long before many of their parents and teachers knew how. As with the printing revolution, the new medium led to massive change across cultural structures, from the organization of work, to politics to medicine, personal relationships, and finally education.

We have some very important decisions to make if we want to truly prepare our children for a world in which the Internet is the dominant media. Continuing our current strategy of filtering the Internet is no longer sufficient. Children need us to be exemplary role models.

The reality is that when many of our children come home from school, they are uploading and downloading videos; they are creating their own Web sites and collaborating with peers. Their Internet searches are not filtered. In fact, as I write this, my high school age son, Dan, is in the basement with six of his friends playing video games with other people from around the world. Dan has the latest Internet video game technology and his friends have flocked to our house to connect with the world. They are operating in multiple windows, plotting mapping strategies, making collaborative and individual decisions, communicating face-to-face and across the Web. The capacity of the game is 32 simultaneous users. It is approaching 11 PM and I will have to ask them to return to their own homes soon.

If it were only about games, we could probably ignore much of what the Internet has to offer. However, as Thomas Freedman so articulately described in his book, *The World Is Flat,* connections around the world are transforming developing countries into hotbeds of engineering and innovation. Those who have the ability to manage massive amounts of information and assemble teams of high-performing workers, regardless of time zones, will have capacity to contribute more to society.

Our students deserve our thoughtful and balanced approach to tapping the Web for their learning. They need us to be role models. We must learn more about why they are so motivated to connect with people around the world. As many schools are choosing to "protect" students from the outside world, students are in turn pushing the limits. They are creating three-dimensional virtual models, using tools like MySpace to collaboratively raise money for worthy charities, and teaching each other using podcasts and screencasts. But as we all know, for as many inspiring stories as there are, there are just as many stories, and more, of students actively plagiarizing the work of others, losing ownership of content they place on MySpace, and unknowingly putting themselves at risk. The decision not to educate our students in this new media is a dangerous one.

After more than 40 years of dominance, television has been replaced by the Internet as the primary media for presidential candidates to raise money and broadcast their messages. The use of blogs, YouTube videos, podcasts, and RSS feeds have become the foundation strategy of how we elect people to the highest office in the land. Yet, if we do not teach our students how to think critically about this media, they will not have the ability to separate the message from the medium. In this regard it is a very dangerous time.

It is also a very exciting time. Like the presidential candidates, educators can harness the power of the Internet to get their message out and to empower students to become more actively involved in managing their own learning. We can teach students critical thinking and how to be socially responsible when they use the Internet to have a globally connected voice. For example, if my son were given the chance to debate students in England about the origins of the American Revolution and his teacher were to record and podcast the debate across iTunes, he would likely be very motivated to prepare for this authentic audience—perhaps much more motivated than preparing for a test on the same subject next Friday. As soon as that podcast is posted in iTunes, he would download it to his iPod for his personal review. Today in many schools, iTunes and global communication tools are blocked, making this kind of rigorous and motivating assignment impossible.

This book was written to help educators prepare students to think critically about the information and communication they use on the Web. There are very clear answers about teaching students the "grammar of the Internet." While you read, I encourage you to think about these questions:

How much control should our schools exert when it comes to providing student access to powerful information and social tools?

How much should we tap these same tools to help students discover their way in a fast-changing world?

Web Basics for Critical Thinking

My own introduction to critical thinking on the Web was the result of a high school student, Zack, handing in a term paper called, "The Historic Myth of Concentration Camps." Of course, the teacher was horrified by her student's lack of discrimination of a source on the Web claiming that the Holocaust was really a medical response to save the Jews from the rampant spread of typhus caused by head lice. This was 1998, when only a few schools had access to the Web. The school's initial response was to punish the student. What made the event intriguing and even more complicated was the address of the Web site: http://pubweb.northwestern.edu/~abutz/intro. This page no longer exists at Northwestern University, but at the time, it was an individual professor's Web page.

When I had a chance to interview the student and asked why he thought the content to be valid, he understandably told me that the Northwestern University address provided the authority he needed to believe the content to be the latest historic research. What he had never learned in school was how to decode a Web address. The tilde (~) character was all the punctuation he needed to know that the address was a personal opinion and not an official document of the university. He had been sent to the Web to find a source, but he was never taught how to validate and cross-reference his sources. The Web has its own punctuation and grammar. It is different, but not much more complicated than the grammar of print and paper. Before we send students to the Web for research, they should be prepared to understand the basic rules of how the content is organized, referenced, and validated. Once our students have a basic grounding in the "grammar of the Internet," they can engage in critical thinking.

The rules of research have changed with society's move from paper to digital information. When we were growing up, we were taught to select our reference content from the library. Our range of content was controlled. Stacks of books with authors, titles, and publishers were easy to find; fiction and nonfiction were clearly organized. Digital technology has changed all that. The old controls are gone. Our students can now find information in reference sources, such as the National Archives, that only scholars would have had access to. In addition, they have a direct connection to a global social network beyond our imaginations. Students can write to specialists directly, post their ideas for debate on the blogs of political commentators in London, and get links from professional journals and podcasts from experts. The potential is mind-boggling.

What this shift of control means is that the role of the teacher is more important than ever. Now it is essential that we teach our children the discipline of making meaning from a very complex and constantly shifting global warehouse of information and communication.

To think critically about the information we accessed, we had to learn the grammar and structure of print information. As we all know, it is essential to know the author of a book, how to use the index, the value of checking footnotes, and to cross-reference. These same steps must also be applied to digital information. It is very important to understand that the Internet has a very different way of organizing information than paper technology. In many ways, there are more skills of cross-referencing to master on the Internet than in the world of paper. Once we learn these skills, we are all in much better command of how information and communication influences our thinking and decision making. For example, if the top search result in Google for the search phrase *"global warming"* is owned by the American Petrolium Institute, it would be important to understand that they may have purchased the key phrase, *"global warming"*, in order to ensure that you would find their Web site at the top of your results. Can you imagine purchasing keywords in the Dewey Decimal System or buying your way to the front of the card catalogue!

In this first chapter, you will be introduced to the basics about thinking critically about Web information. The basics begin with an understanding of the structure of the Web, its punctuation, and its grammar.

The contents of this chapter are elementary to understanding how the Web works and how it is organized. The purpose is to provide you with some clear definitions and practical ideas to learn and teach the basics of the Internet to your students. It is the first step toward Web literacy and critical thinking. Let the adventure begin.

THE ESSENTIALS

What Is the Internet?

The Internet is a network of many different computers, all over the world, connected together. The network allows computers to talk to each other even though they may be separated by large distances, are made by different manufacturers, and run on different kinds of operating systems.

IP Addresses

The Internet works by allowing Web browsers (software for retrieving Web pages) to call up addresses, much like ordinary mail. These addresses are called Internet protocol (IP) addresses. An example of such an address might be 212.58.240.33.

Are your eyes glazing over? Not to worry. You normally do not see an address written in this numeric form while browsing the Web. Instead you will see text with slashes and dots like this: http://www.cnn.com/. Every IP address also has a corresponding domain name. This makes remembering and navigating to Web sites much easier.

Domain Names

In the CNN Web address, *cnn.com* is the *domain name*. A domain name can have two or possibly three components. The first component is created by the owner of a site. No one can create a name if it has already been assigned to someone else. For example, the rights to use the domain *cnn.com* have already been purchased. Nobody else can use that domain name unless CNN decides they no longer wish to purchase the rights.

The second component is called a TLD, or *top level domain*, and is designated for certain groups or categories. Examples of these categories are *.com* for commercial, *.gov* for government, and *.edu* for educational sites. If navigating to a site that is hosted in another country there will be an additional extension, called a country code. For example, *.uk* refers to the United Kingdom.

Component one examples	Component two examples	Country code examples
nike	.k12	.au (Australia)
cnn	.com	.ca (Canada)
mnh.si	.edu	.ch (Switzerland)
endangeredspecies	.ac	.cn (China)
nfl	.mil	.de (Germany)
nasa	.org	.es (Spain)
travel	.gov	.et (Ethiopia)
	.net	.fr (France)
	.sch	.gr (Greece)
	.biz	.ie (Ireland)
		.in (India)
		.iq (Iraq)
		.il (Israel)
		.it (Italy)
		.jp (Japan)
		.mx (Mexico)
		.nz (New Zealand)
		.uk (United Kingdom)
		.us (United States)
		.za (South Africa)

When you put all the components together you get domain names that look like these:

sahistory.org.za

kiwirecovery.org.nz

culture.gr

tv-tokyo.co.jp

Many Web sites contain two components, a word and an extension (*novemberlearning.com*), but some contain a third component (support .microsoft.com). This third component is a *subdomain*. A subdomain always has a dot separating it from the other components. In the previous example, *support* is the subdomain.

Buying Domain Names

People often select domain names very carefully. In essence, they represent the Web site to the outside world. Typically people want a domain name that describes who they are, such as adidas.com. At times, however, people use their domain name to manipulate and hide the true purpose of their site. For example, MartinLutherKing.org is a site published by a white supremacist group dedicated to the abolition of Martin Luther King, Jr., Day. You might not assume that by looking at the domain name, but further research will quickly show that this site is actually owned by an organization called Stormfront, which promotes white pride.

For Students—What's in a Domain Name?

A California-based nonprofit organization named ICANN currently manages the assignments of Internet addresses. The rights to a domain name are purchased from registration companies. Register.com and EasyDNS.com are examples of two companies that have the commercial licence to sell you a Web address. You can go to either of these sites, or many others like them, to search any domain name you wish in order to see if it is available for purchase.

For example, *harrypotter.com* was purchased by the film company, Warner Brothers. The domain *nike.com* is being used by the sporting goods company, Nike. In many ways, selecting a domain name is a way for Web site owners to advertise, but for others, it's a way to manipulate and draw you in. For example, the Web address http://www.martinlutherking.org/ is not owned by a nonprofit group called the Martin Luther King Organization. As we mentioned before, it is owned by a white supremacist group promoting white pride worldwide and called Stormfront.

URLs

Another useful bit of Internet jargon is *URL*, which is simply another term for Web address. URL stands for Uniform Resource Locator.

World Wide Web

Most URLs begin with *www.*, which stands for *World Wide Web*. The World Wide Web is a collection of billions of Web pages stored on computers called servers. These pages can contain text, graphics, video, and sound. As with a catalogue or book, these pages usually relate to a common theme or subject. Most are written in a computer language called Hypertext Markup Language (HTML). The good news is you don't need to know HTML in order to read the Web; it works in the background, organizing the presentation of the page.

When you type a URL into your Web browser and hit enter, the browser sends a request to the server that stores the page. The server then sends the page to your browser and it appears on your computer screen.

Web Browsers

A browser is a computer program that lets you *browse* the Internet for information. It retrieves data from remote servers and displays Web pages. Some popular browsers are Internet Explorer, Netscape Navigator, Safari, and Firefox.

Home Pages

When you first type a domain name into your browser, the first place you usually arrive is the site's *home page*. The home page can act like an index or the front cover of a book or magazine, linking to further information. It may contain links to other pages on the same site, or pages to other Web sites.

√ Try This

Do not be surprised if you type in a URL and are redirected to another address that looks far different from the one you have entered. Chances are the URL is *forwarded*, meaning it points to another address. Companies often have several addresses that all lead to the same site. For example, if you enter *www.harrypotter.com* into a browser, you will be redirected to this page: http://www.harrypotterorderofthephoenix.com/. Try it and see.

Links

Links are a powerful concept. They enable you to easily surf the Web and navigate through related sources of information with split-second connections. For example, you can click on a map in a Web site and instantly be transported to a video camera that shows that part of the world in real time. To the knowledgeable user, links are a powerful research tool; they empower you to harness information and quickly solve problems. Links can also be enormously distracting. Within seconds, you can be led to inappropriate or misleading material. Teaching students how to tame the power of links is an important skill.

Links are usually underlined, highlighted, or represented by a graphic. In most browsers, by moving a cursor over a link, the cursor arrow will turn into a hand and a URL will appear in the status bar at the lower left of your browser.

> **√ Try This**
>
> Go to http://www.thebritishmuseum.ac.uk and rest your cursor over several of the links. Look to see how your cursor changes and where the URL appears on the lower left of your browser. This is a validating trick we will refer to later.

EXPLORING THE GRAMMAR OF THE INTERNET

Michael's Story

I have shown sixth grade social studies classes the "Victorian Robots" site on several occasions. It's a historical site about robots built in the Victorian era. You see pictures of a robot with Pancho Villa and at various historical events. It's very clever. (Similar to Forrest Gump meeting with President Kennedy.) As I go through the links with students, show the pictures, and ask them what they think, the majority are believers. The photographs are very convincing. I even read that historians have been fooled by this site. It's fascinating to me that not one of my students has ever commented on the URL. It's not until I point it out and show them the home page to see who has published the information that they realize they've been tricked. Reading a Web address is totally off their radar—definitely not something they think about. Yet, it is so simple, like reading the title of a book.

We spend a great deal of time teaching students how to find print information in a library—it's just as important to teach them how information is organized on the Web. Knowing a thing or two about the architecture of a Web address is crucial. All those dots and dashes in a URL are meaningful. They are an important part of the grammar of the Internet. Just as a number or letter on the spine of a book in the library is important—so is the grammar of a Web page.

Reading a Web address is often essential to establishing the authenticity of a Web site. A URL can sometimes tell you plenty about a site, or in some cases, nothing at all.

How to Read a URL

Any given URL can provide you with a snapshot of how Web pages within that site are organized. Along with the domain name, a URL describes specific folders, servers, companies, countries, and communication methods. Sound confusing? It's not really. Here are some examples.

Example 1: http://www.moma.org/

This URL from the Museum of Modern Art is the home page of the site. In the domain name, *moma.org*, *moma* refers to Museum of Modern Art. The extension, *.org*, refers to an organization. Be aware. Organization is loosely defined. Anyone with a credit card can purchase a Web address with a .org extension.

Example 2: http://www.moma.org/education/

This URL leads to a Web page that includes the same domain name, but is deeper in the moma site. There can be thousands of pages on a Web site. Each slash (/) in a URL represents another level deeper, like a folder within a folder.

Example 3: http://www.sandiegozoo.org/ teachers/classroom_activities.html

Some really long URLs will have many forward slashes. An example is this page from the San Diego Zoo. Each forward slash on this URL represents one level deeper into the site. In this example, *classroom_activities.html* is a file in the *teachers* folder, and *teachers* is a folder within the site sandiegozoo.org.

√ Try This

- Web addresses are read left to right.
- Unlike in books, there are no page numbers. The way you find a specific page on a site is to have the right address that points to the one page you are looking for.
- There are no spaces in URLs.
- Slashes are always forward (/).

Truncating a URL

What's nice about the structure of URLs is that you can check out the page or level above the one from which you started. It can be a great trick when validating information. Truncating is done by clicking at the end of a Web address and deleting all characters up to the previous left slash. Each time you delete to the previous slash, you move up a level in the organization of the site. You can delete right to left until you finally end up with just the domain name—which is generally the home page of a site.

√ Try This

Truncate this URL. Start with the top address and remove one level at a time:
http://www.sandiegozoo.org/teachers/classroom_activities.html
http://www.sandiegozoo.org/teachers/
http://www.sandiegozoo.org/

Victorian Robots

A home page can sometimes give you perspective about a site or help you find more information. As Michael pointed out in his story, it can also be a validating tool. If you are ever concerned about the quality of information on a site, try looking at its home page. Just as you might judge a book by its cover, you can sometimes judge a Web site by its home page.

For Students—Victorian Robots

This site is an excellent example to use with students when demonstrating how to truncate a URL to find out more information about the authenticity of Web site information. Try it with *http://bigredhair.com/robots/index.html.*

Might your students also believe that a Victorian robot spent time with Pancho Villa and fought in World War I, and that the photographs are authentic? Probably not after they see the home page.

For Students

This exercise might be a good starting point for younger students when introducing some of the concepts introduced in this chapter. Here are two other popular sites to show students and for you to preview. Have students decide whether the two sites are related in any way. If so, how are they related?

Site #1: The Pacific Northwest Tree Octopus (http://zapatopi.net/treeoctopus/)
Site #2: Bureau of Sasquatch Affairs (http://zapatopi.net/bsa/)

Both sites are fictitious, but note they share the same domain name, zapatopi.net, which means they were published by the same person or company. If you truncate the URLs of both sites, you will end up at the same home page.

CONCLUSION

This chapter has introduced some basic vocabulary and essential tenets of the grammar of the Internet. Although some of what you have read may have been elementary, these are the building blocks for critical thinking on the Web and the first steps toward becoming Web literate. Knowing the architecture of a URL and how to truncate and recognize domain names and extensions will be skills referred to throughout the course of this book.

RESOURCES

British Museum (http://www.thebritishmuseum.ac.uk/)

Bureau of Sasquatch Affairs (http://zapatopi.net/bsa/)

CNN (http://www.cnn.com/)

Harry Potter (http://www.harrypotter.com/)

Museum of Modern Art (http://www.moma.org/)

The Pacific Northwest Tree Octopus (http://zapatopi.net/treeoctopus/)

San Diego Zoo (http://www.sandiegozoo.org/teachers/classroom_activities.html)

Victorian Robots (http://bigredhair.com/robots/index.html)

ASSESSMENT

1. What is the Internet?
   a. An assortment of ideas over the Web
   b. A network of many different computers connected together
   c. A server
   d. A Web browser

2. A link allows you to:
   a. Make notes about the information on a Web page
   b. Access a formal reference to an information source
   c. Instantly connect to another Web page

3. What is the home page of a Web site?
   a. The starting point of a Web site, almost like the front cover of a book or magazine
   b. Where a Web author must list his or her credentials
   c. The best page of a Web site

4. What two things happen when you place your cursor over a link?
    a. You return to the home page and back to the domain name.
    b. Your cursor turns into an arrow and the URL of the link appears in the lower left of your screen.
    c. Your cursor turns into a hand and the URL of the link appears in the lower left of your screen.

5. A URL:
    a. Is the same as an IP address, but much easier to remember than a list of numbers.
    b. Is also known as a Web address.
    c. Contains a domain name.
    d. All of the above.

6. Which of the following is NOT an example of a domain name?
    a. nyu.edu
    b. cnn.ext
    c. novemberlearning.com
    d. whitehouse.gov

7. A domain name:
    a. Can sometimes tell you about the Web browser you are using.
    b. May be designed to fool you about the actual content of the site.
    c. Will never contain an extension.
    d. Tells you absolutely nothing about the content of a site—ever.

8. How do you truncate a Web address?
    a. Remove the domain name from the URL.
    b. Remove the *http://* or the *www.* from a URL.
    c. Remove levels from the URLs right to left until you are left with the domain name.
    d. None of the above.

9. What is the purpose of truncating a URL?
    a. To help navigate through a Web site.
    b. To help find the home page of a Web site.
    c. To help find more information on a Web site.
    d. All of the above.

10. Read the URLs below and identify the domain name within each.
    http://www.thebritishmuseum.ac.uk/compass/
    http://educationworld.com/a_tech/archives/interactivity.shtml
    http://www.cnn.com/TECH/
    http://www.shakespeare.com/Poetry/ieindex.html

11. What is the domain name of this URL? http://educationworld
    .com/a_tech/archives/interactivity.shtml
    a. educationworld.com
    b. .shtml
    c. .com
    d. http://

12. Companies often select domain names designed to draw people to
    their Web site. True or false?

13. Truncating a Web address is not a method of validating Web site
    information. True or false?

Answer Key: 1. b; 2. c; 3. a; 4. c; 5. d; 6. b; 7. b; 8. c; 9. d; 10. thebritish
museum.ac.uk, educationworld.com, cnn.com, shakespeare.com; 11. a;
12. True; 13. False

QUESTIONS FOR EXTENDED THOUGHT AND DISCUSSION

1. If you believe that all students should be Web literate, what is
   the best strategy for your school or district to prepare students with
   this skill?

2. What skills should all teachers have to be Web literate?

3. What role should school filtering play in your school district? Who
   should make this decision?

4. Do you believe the Internet is as big a transformer of culture as
   the printing press?

5. If yes, what parts of our culture do you believe will be most affected?

The Empowered Researcher

Rob's Story

I do a lot of computer training for staff, students, and teaching interns. The most common trends I see with young people using search engines are that most will only click on the first few results and that the only search engines people ever seem to use are Google and Yahoo!

Once I was training with some teacher interns and was helping someone find information on magnetic declination. She needed to know how to use a compass for a project. I watched her conduct a search in Yahoo! for compass. The Web site for REI sporting goods came up on top as a "Sponsor Result" so she clicked on it without realizing she was being misled. I see this all the time. Many people are not aware of paid listings on Web sites. Anyone with deep pockets can get to the top of a results list by purchasing key search terms. That's why I try to spend as much time as possible coaching people on how to frame their searches for better results. For example, I showed her that if she changed her keyword search to the phrases *"how to read a compass"* or *"magnetic declination"* and ignored the many sponsored results, that she would find a much more targeted list of usable results. Knowing what to ask the search engine to do is critical—and so is understanding how a search engine works.

Knowing how search engines work and how they can manipulate results will make experiences with the Internet safer, easier, and more productive. In this chapter, you will learn about different types of search engines, be introduced to tools available to educators, and learn ways you might be misled by the way search results are ranked.

HOW DO SEARCH ENGINES WORK?

Search engines collect information about World Wide Web content by using programs called *robots* or *spiders.* These programs are automated browsers that roam the Web and collect information such as text, titles of pages, and meta-tags from documents. (Meta-tags are words a Web author uses to describe his or her page.) Information is pulled into a search engine database, where it is indexed into smaller chunks of information.

When you conduct a search, your keywords are matched against the search engine database. Results are sent back as pages of links. Search engines do not search the entire Web at the moment you enter keywords into the search box. They only search within their own databases. That is why your results appear so quickly. In some cases it takes weeks for a new Web site to appear in a search engine's database.

Search engines do not all work the same way. When roaming the Web, some focus more on pages, and some crawl the Web more often. Others evaluate keywords differently or count the number of links going in or out of a site. Additionally, different search engines serve different purposes. For example, Technorati is a search engine that searches only within blog postings, while Podscope searches for audio and video.

Is One Better Than Another?

Think of it this way: when you go shopping, chances are you will head to the store most likely to have what you are looking for. Whether you need hardware, groceries, clothes, or appliances—certain stores are appropriate for your needs, be it a speciality shop or a department store. Search engines are relatively the same. Whether you are looking for an image of a whale, historical archive about Abraham Lincoln, audio file, teacher resource, Web log, or podcast, there are "specialty" search tools specific for each need. If you are looking for information in general or a quick fact, you might just choose a regular search engine—a virtual warehouse of information. Whatever it is you are looking for, the following are some examples of different search tools from which to choose and try with your students.

Use Your Noodle

NoodleTools offers a wide selection of search tools specific to certain needs and prompts users to focus a research query. Prompts such as "I need to see relationships among ideas," or "I need a subject hub prepared by an expert" help direct students to the right place and get them thinking critically about what they are trying to achieve.

NoodleTools (http://www.noodletools.com/debbie/literacies/information/5locate/adviceengine.html). Choose the best search for your information needs.

NoodleQuest (http://www.noodletools.com/noodlequest/). This site is an interactive version of the one listed above.

Kid-Centric

The two search engines below are perfect to use with younger students. The search tools contained within both are geared toward a younger audience.

Tek Mom's Search Tools for Students (http://www.tekmom.com/search/). Tekmom has assembled a good assortment of search tools and databases.

Ivy's Search Engine Resources for Kids (http://www.ivyjoy.com/rayne/kidssearch.html). This is a great site for students because so many search tools are available on one page.

For Those Interested in Higher-Level Scholarly Material

As students mature, so does their need for more scholarly material. Google provides a terrific search tool for just that purpose.

Google Scholar (http://www.scholar.google.com/). Provides higher-level student researchers with material from scholarly resources.

Electronic Textbooks

It pays to become familiar with the databases that house content-specific information in your subject area, such as historic primary documents or scientific information. Many of these databases are available on the deep Web. In many ways, these databases are like an electronic textbook and can provide much better information than a regular search on the Web. For example:

NASAKids (http://kids.msfc.nasa.gov/)

Sea World Animal Information Database (http://www.seaworld.org/Search/query.htm)

Directories

Yahoo! is an example of a directory. They are searchable indexes where people instead of Web robots compile collections of resources. In a directory, you enter the title of a site you are looking for and it will return as many related links as it can locate.

Meta-Searching

Meta-search engines collect and correlate top results from other search engines. They basically search several major search engines all at once. Examples include Dogpile and Web Crawler.

Tapping the World of Blogs

You may have heard of blogs, or Web logs. If you haven't you will soon. A blog is an interactive Web page where individuals can post entries, articles, links, and pictures, and ask others to join into conversations. For educators, they are a way to expand the boundaries of learning. Teachers can post entries for students, for parents, and for professional development purposes. Students can engage with others in their community or around the world and post their work to an authentic audience.

Blogs are relatively simple to use and very popular. New search engines are dedicated to searching the Web in real time to find out what is going on in the world of blogs. Currently the biggest ones of the bunch are Technorati (http://www.technorati.com/) and Google Blog Search (http://blogsearch.google.com/).

Please note that searching through blogs is not a wise choice for students looking for academic information. Blogs are largely personal accounts and subject to bias. Plus, a lot of them contain very inappropriate content. If there is a blog you would like your students to see, we recommend that you find it first. Ideas for searching for blogs for educational use might include:

- Find other teachers in your subject area and/or level that have one. This is a great way to find resources you might want to use, or establish a blog connection between classes.
- Find scholars or authors in a particular field.

Tuning In to Podcasts

Podcasts are audio or video content that can be downloaded or fed to a mobile music player (MP3 player or iPod). Podcasting allows anyone to create and self-publish a syndicated "radio show" and gives broadcast radio or television programs a new way to distribute content. This technology is rather new at the moment and search engines are starting to pop up. Try:

Podscope (http://www.podscope.com/)

Blinkx (http://www.blinkx.com/)

Everyzing (http://www.everyzing.com/)

Another option here would be to use iTunes. It's actually a software program that you download and install onto your computer and is currently the easiest way to search for and subscribe to podcasts. Go to http://www.apple.com/itunes/ to find the free download.

WHO CONTROLS INFORMATION ON THE INTERNET?

Although some amazing resources can be found on the Web, each time you use a search engine, you need to ask yourself, "Why did these results pop up?"

As Rob pointed out at the beginning of this chapter, one of the most common things he notices when doing computer training is how often people click on sites that appear at the top of a list of results. Watch when your students do research—chances are you will see a similar trend. Because we are more likely to click on the top of a list results, the ranking of search engine results is a lucrative business and something that is monitored very closely.

For Sale! The English Language

You can bid on any keyword search term you wish at a search marketing company, such as Yahoo! Some are more costly than others. For example, you might find that a keyword like *Elvis* costs about 30 cents. Another, such as the phrase *"breast cancer"*, can be up to $3. That means that the person who bids the price has to pay if someone clicks on their site. For example, when the teacher intern clicked on the REI sporting goods site when searching for information on compasses during Rob's training session, REI paid 60 cents.

Yahoo! estimates that in the United States more than 300 million times per day a keyword is entered into a search engine. Fifty percent of these searches are looking for a particular product or service. Considering these statistics, it's no wonder advertisers are interested in tapping into the search engine market.

If a keyword has been bid on and you conduct a search using that word, your search results will begin with a *sponsored search.* (Different search engines use different terms.) As Rob mentioned, many students and adults don't realize that sites rank at the top because they've paid to be there. It's not that these sites are necessarily bad; you just can't assume they offer top quality information if you or your students are looking for academic-type information. They are often trying to sell you something or make you think a certain way, which may mean they are subject to bias. For example, during one U.S. presidential election, the phrase *global warming* was purchased by the American Petroleum Institute. *Social Security* was another hot phrase being purchased during a recent election.

International Marketing

It is worth noting that search engines operate separately within different countries. Marketers have the ability to bid for keywords either regionally or worldwide. In other words, keywords that are bid on in the United Kingdom may only appear as sponsored listings on designated U.K. search engines. The same holds true for the United States.

A False Sense of Security

Just because paid listings are grouped in a specific section with a clear heading does not mean that the rest of your results are safe from manipulation. Not a chance. Understanding how a search engine ranks results may surprise you. For example, take Google. Google is currently the most popular search engine used. It is so popular, in fact, that it has its own infinitive verb, *to google,* and its own affliction, *Googlitis.* Googlitis is an affliction that strikes students and adults who rely on this search engine wholeheartedly and fail to question how it generates results!

When you enter a keyword into Google, your search results are pulled together and organized using a highly sophisticated mathematical algorithm. This algorithm takes into account numerous factors including, but not limited to, the actual domain name, the title of the Web site, the meta-information contained within the background of the site, the actual text on the page, and the number of links coming into that site from others. Once all of these factors are measured and plugged into Google's algorithm, you are presented with a page of search results. What this means is that the results of your search do not necessarily have anything to do with the quality of the information. A site at the top might be there based on how many links are coming into it from other sites. Popularity does not equal the best quality.

What is most interesting about this process is that many of these factors can be controlled by a savvy Web page creator whose intentions might not be to get you the most reliable information. For example, if you type the keyword *octopus* into Google, the Save the Pacific Northwest Tree Octopus site (http://www.zapatopi.net/treeoctopus) will be near the top of your results. Careful reading of this site will quickly indicate that the information on this site is a hoax. It is certainly not an authentic resource for students researching octopi.

For Students—Evaluating Search Engines

The purpose of this exercise is for students to see how different search engines rank sites given the same keyword search. Are the top results in one search engine "better" than another?

Divide the class into groups and assign each group four different search engines. If your students are younger, be sure to select child-oriented search engines, such as the science search engine at http://whyfiles.org/ from the University of Wisconsin. Provide each group with a list of research keywords specific to your subject area or a current news event—for example, the keyword, *octopus*. Make sure your words do not have any double meanings that might solicit inappropriate results.

Suggested sites:

Tekmom (http://www.tekmom.com/search/): There are many sites to choose from.

Ivy's resource centre for kids (http://www.ivyjoy.com/rayne/kidssearch.html)

Google (http://www.google.com/)

Ask.com (http://www.ask.com/)

Answers.com (http://www.answers.com/)

Lycos (http://www.lycos.com/)

AltaVista (http://www.altavista.com/)

HotBot.com (http://www.hotbot.com/)

Yahooligans (http://yahooligans.yahoo.com/)

Dogpile (http://www.dogpile.com/)

(Continued)

(Continued)

WebCrawler (http://www.webcrawler.com/)

AlltheWeb (http://www.alltheweb.com/)

Ask students to try a search with the same keyword in their four search engines. Have them record the top five results for each, plus count the number of paid listings per each search, and answer these questions.

- Compare and contrast the results from the various engines. Can you make any generalizations?
- Did some search engines seem to have more paid listings than others? If so, which ones?
- Which search engines might you be more likely to use and why?
- How might using more than one search engine when researching information help you find better information?
- What conclusions can you draw about researching information on the Internet?

Students should realize they need to use more than one search engine when they do research. They should also look past the top results.

They may wish to refer to UC Berkeley's BEST search engines site (http://www.lib.berkeley.edu/TeachingLib/Guides/Internet/SearchEngines.html) for information on how particular search engines work.

Have students present their Web sites and findings.

Google in the United States Compared With Google in China

Much has been written about how the results from Google in China can be different than what you might find in the United States. Try logging on to http://www.langreiter.com/exec/google-vs-google.html to see an immediate comparison between the two countries. Type in *"free speech"* or *capitalism.* Move your cursor over the blue and white dots on both the American and Chinese version of results to see how the two versions of results differ. Ask your students to explain why Google's results might differ in two different countries.

CONCLUSION

From compasses to podcasts, the Internet is the largest warehouse of information in the world. Knowing how to access the "good stuff" comes with knowing how the search engines work and how all the pieces fit together. Using critical-thinking skills when using a search engines is just the beginning. In the next chapter we move toward validating information—what to do with the information once you actually find it.

RESOURCES

AlltheWeb (http://www.alltheweb.com/)

AltaVista (http://www.altavista.com/)

Answers.com (http://www.answers.com/)

Ask.com (http://www.ask.com/)

Blinkx (http://www.blinkx.com/)

Dogpile (http://www.dogpile.com/)

Everyzing (http://www.everyzing.com/)

Google (http://www.google.com/)

HotBot.com (http://www.hotbot.com/)

Ivy's resource centre for kids (http://www.ivyjoy.com/rayne/kidssearch.html)

Lycos (http://www.lycos.com/)

NASAKids (http://kids.msfc.nasa.gov/)

Noodletools (http://www.noodletools.com/debbie/literacies/information/5locate/adviceengine.html)

NoodleQuest (http://www.noodletools.com/noodlequest/)

Podscope (http://www.podscope.com/)

Sea World Animal Information Database (http://www.seaworld.org/Search/query.htm)

Technorati (http://www.technorati.com/)

Tekmom (http://www.tekmom.com/search/)

UC Berkeley's BEST search engines (http://www.lib.berkeley.edu/TeachingLib/Guides/Internet/SearchEngines.html)

WebCrawler (http://www.webcrawler.com/)

Yahoo! (http://www.yahoo.com/)

Yahooligans (http://yahooligans.yahoo.com/)

ASSESSMENT

1. If the quality of content is not in the search engine's algorithm, then what is?
   a. Links coming into a Web site from somewhere else
   b. The title of the Web site
   c. The URL of the Web site
   d. All of the above

2. In what ways can search results be manipulated?
   a. You tell all of your friends to link to your site.
   b. Many search results begin with sponsored listings, which means people pay to have their listing appear at the top of your results.
   c. All of the above.
   d. None of the above.

3. Search results between Yahoo! and Google are consistently the same. True or false?

4. Why do companies purchase search keywords?
   a. To create more business
   b. To get their site to the top of your results list
   c. To fool you into thinking they have something more to offer
   d. To make money from the search engine
   e. All of the above
   f. Both a and c
   g. Both a and b

5. Who pays when you click the title of a Sponsored Link or Sponsored Match?
   a. The search engine company
   b. The company whose title you have clicked

6. A Sponsored Link or Sponsored Match that appears in the United States will automatically appear in another country, such as Australia. True or false?

7. Why is it important for students NOT to research academic information from sponsored links or sponsored matches?
   a. Researching from these sites is fine.
   b. Information on those pages is subject to bias.
   c. Just because a site has paid to be at the top of results list doesn't mean it has the best information.
   d. Many of these types of sites are trying to sell you something.
   e. All of the above.

f. a, b, and c

g. b, c, and d

Answer Key: 1. d; 2. b; 3. False; 4. g; 5. b; 6. False; 7. g

QUESTIONS FOR EXTENDED THOUGHT AND DISCUSSION

1. What is your favorite search engine and why?

2. Can you imagine how to use the sale of keywords into a lesson?

3. Do you believe the Internet will influence how people vote?

4. When using the same search engine around the world, you can see very different results with the same search phrases, such as *"global warming"* or *Tibet.* What impact do you think this will have on global understanding?

Get REAL

How to Validate Information on the Web

As you recall from Chapter 1, a student named Zack handed in a term paper explaining the holocaust as an historic myth. If Zack had been prepared to decode the grammar of the Northwestern University Web site about the Holocaust, he would have had a chance to question the information presented to him.

In Zack's case, neither he nor the faculty at his school had an understanding of Internet grammar, syntax, and cross-referencing. Under these conditions, it is understandable that the immediate response of the teacher and the school was deep disappointment in the student. The student was blamed for a lack of critical thinking. He was taught to use a search engine, but was not taught to think critically about the information he found.

His research for the paper came from a Web page at Northwestern University. The site, written by Arthur Butz, was an essay called, "A Short Introduction to the Study of Holocaust Revisionism." Again, the URL was http://pubweb.northwestern.edu/~abutz/di/intro.html.

On his Web page, Butz explained that he wrote "A Short Introduction to the Study of Holocaust Revisionism" and that his material was intended for "advanced students of Holocaust revisionism." At the top of the page he identified himself as "Associate Professor of Electrical and Computer Engineering, Northwestern University."

Furthermore, Butz suggested that concentration camps were an attempt by the German government to help the Jews fight typhus carried by lice, and that the death camps were really medical clinics. He did not deny the shaving and showers, the canisters of the gas Zyklon, the crematoria, and deaths. He simply explained these details as necessary actions for the eradication of lice. (As a point of information, head lice do not transmit disease.)

Consider Zack. He's 14 and untrained to think critically about Web information. He is researching the Holocaust and by searching for the name of one of the chemicals used in the gas chambers, Zyklon, he finds Professor Butz's Web page. He thought he had found academic information perfect for his paper. He recognized *northwestern* in the domain name of the Web address and the extension *.edu* (*.edu* in a Web address refers to a higher educational site).

The Web page was simple and clear; it was written in a calm, logical tone. From a student perspective, the page was intended for experts in this area of research. Best of all, the source was from a professor from a premiere university. What more could a 14-year-old researcher ask for?

Zack was doing his research on the Holocaust at home when he found the Arthur Butz site. Many schools filter sites such as this one using expensive Web filtering tools, but most families with home computers do not have these filtering systems. Generally, students are on the Web at home, away from the "protection" of schools and their advanced filters. Ironically, in Zack's situation, he could have accessed this site from his school. Since the information was at a local research university, his school's filter was not blocking it.

Zack's story presents a prime example of why we need to teach children to think critically about and validate information found on the Web. Too often, students accept information that looks authentic as the "truth," and this is one of the dangers of the Web. They need to be aware that *anyone* can publish *anything* they want. It is not enough to tell children to be wary about the information they read on the Web. We need to go further and provide them with real tools and skills to help them think critically about what they are reading.

As the school learned more about how they did not prepare Zack to deal with any version of the truth on the Web, they challenged him to interview a holocaust survivor. As every educator knows, it is always important to have different sources of reference.

At a leadership conference at Stanford, I had the opportunity to interview a holocaust survivor about his thoughts in reference to the Arthur Butz site. I asked him how the education community should respond to a revisionist site. As a college professor, he was very articulate and absolutely confident about his answer, "Students must be made aware of sites like this so they cannot be misled." He went on to explain that it would be the role of a teacher to guide students to a balance of sources: Stories of holocaust survivors, records kept by the Germans during World War II, and soldiers who liberated the camps.

GET REAL

A simple scaffold to help students validate Web materials is a four-step process called REAL. REAL is a short and easy acronym to remember. Each step involves a set of skills and concepts that can be learned by anyone.

It's unlikely that students will go through each of these steps every time they review a Web site. However, having a grasp of the tools and the rationale behind each will empower any user to thoroughly investigate the authenticity of a Web site.

Once students know the aspects of each step, they will be better equipped to think critically about materials on the Web. They can start by asking, "Is this information REAL?"

STEP 1. READ THE URL

Finding information on the Web is completely different than searching for a book in the library. A book in the library clearly displays the author's and publisher's name, along with when it was written. It's organized in stacks alphabetically or by the Dewey Decimal System.

Web sites are less clear with this type of referential information. You do not always know the author, the publisher, or how long ago the information was updated. And most important, because anyone could be an author, you cannot always trust what you read. People might pretend to be an expert on a topic when really they are not. There is no fiction or nonfiction area of the Internet.

Although a site may or may not appear to be authentic, one of the most expedient ways to find out is to glance at its address. Knowing how to recognize bits of information in the URL may provide information or clues about a site, its publisher, and its relationship to other sites. For example, have a close look at the URL of the site in the Zack story: http://pubweb.northwestern.edu/~abutz/di/intro.html.

There are some important things to note in this Web address. The first is the domain name: northwestern.edu. The name *northwestern* refers to a particular university and the extension *.edu* confirms that it is an institution of higher learning. (Outside of the United States, the extension generally used in college and university Web sites is *.ac.*)

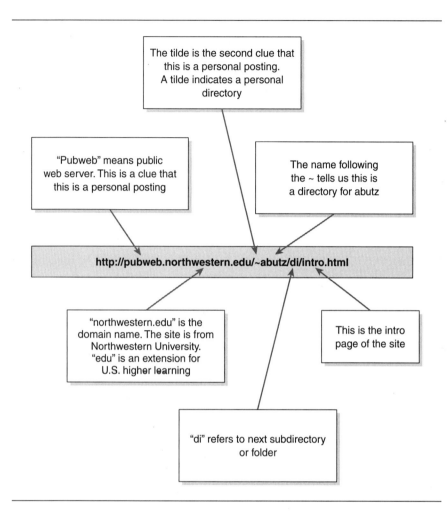

The next items of note are the word *pubweb,* which refers to a public Web server, and the tilde (~), followed by the name, *abutz.* These bits of information provide the biggest clues that this Web site is not an official academic page from Northwestern University, but actually a personal posting.

Students should understand that even though Web sites that contain personal postings can hold accurate information, they should hold these sites suspect. Information from such sites is more likely to contain bias.

What to Look for When Reading a URL

You should ask three basic questions when reading a URL.

Question 1: Do you recognize the domain name?

The domain name can sometimes provide clues about the quality of information or tell you what a site is about.

Question 2: What is the extension in the domain name?

These tiny bits of information are an important part of domain names because they show the type of establishment that owns the domain. Here is a list of things to look for.

COMMON EXTENSIONS

.k12	Schools in the United States (not all U.S. schools use this)
.edu	Educational organization (most U.S. colleges)
.ac	Academic institution (not used in the United States)
.com	Commercial
.org	Any organization
.gov	Government agency
.net	Network
.mil	Military institution (United States)

Some extensions may provide more reliable information than others, but there are no guarantees. Safe bets might be *.edu, .gov, .k12,* and *.sch* (some schools outside of the United States use this one). These extensions can only be obtained and used by educational institutions or government organizations. Ones to be on the lookout for are *.com, .org.,* and *.net.* These extensions can be owned by anybody.

Question 3: Are you on a personal page?

If you do not recognize the domain name or extension of a URL, keep reading past the first forward slash for more clues to see if you are on a personal page.

Look for the following clues:

A name (such as *abutz*)

Tilde (~)

Percent sign (%)

The words *users, people,* or *members*

Remember, as said before, that many personal pages contain useful information or links to important resources and helpful facts. Just keep in mind that personal pages sometimes offer biased opinions.

For Students—Find the Extension

Here's an exercise to try with students to get them thinking about URLs. Use the sample URLs below or invent your own.

Student Instructions

In the following URLs, find the extension in the domain name. What does each extension mean? Without visiting each, what can you tell about the site from just reading the domain name?

1. http://www.nike.com/
2. http://www.si.edu/
3. http://www.sandiegozoo.org/
4. http://news.bbc.co.uk/
5. http://www.seaworld.com/
6. http://www.cam.ac.uk/
7. http://www.upeg.edu/~user/

Answers:

1. The extension is *.com*. The extension tells you it is a commercial site. You can tell this is the home page for the sporting goods store Nike.

2. The extension is *.edu*. The extension tells you it is a higher learning site from the United States. In this case, *si* refers to the Smithsonian Institution. This is their home page.

3. The extension is *.org*. The extension tells you it is an organization. You can tell that this is the home page of the San Diego Zoo.

4. The extension is *.co.uk*. The extension tells you it is a commercial site from the United Kingdom. You can tell that this is the BBC's home page.

5. The extension is *.com*. The extension tells you it is a commercial site and has something to do with Sea World.

6. The extension is *.ac.uk*. The extension tells you it is an academic site from the United Kingdom. This is Cambridge University's home page.

7. The extension is *.edu*. The extension tells you this is a U.S. higher learning site. The tilde and the word *user* tell you this is a personal page.

What Does Northwestern Have to Say?

You may be interested in knowing that the Butz site has caused a great deal of controversy for Northwestern University. At the following URL is a copy of the release put out by Northwestern University in regards to Professor Butz's site: http://www.ibiblio.org/team/history/controversy/970107-Butz.html.

Based on this release, you may be wondering why Professor Butz's site is no longer hosted at Northwestern. As it turns out, Northwestern decided that they would no longer host these open personal pages. According to a response I received from writing to Northwestern, this decision was not in any way related to Professor Butz.

For Students

You may want to consider these discussion questions with your students:

Is the value of intellectual freedom more important than protecting society from views that are contemptible?

At what point does the protection of intellectual freedom outweigh protection of the truth?

What actions would you take if you were the president of the university?

STEP 2. EXAMINE THE CONTENT

Debbie's Story

I have been using the Pacific Northwest Tree Octopus site extensively before many seventh grade classes. The reaction of almost all of the kids (as well as some of the teachers) to this site has been instructive. Despite a discussion about octopi . . . some kids have eaten it, many have seen one in a fish market or aquarium, this site was accepted with great seriousness. Most students agreed that this would be a good source of information for a science report on endangered species. The photograph was especially potent. There was a real disconnect between their actual knowledge and experience, and what they were willing to accept because they saw it on the 'net.

Some very convincing Web sites exist that have been specifically designed to stump readers. They are fun and beautifully done, but their facts are questionable at best. Such Web sites are great tools for teachers to use to help students think critically about the content of Web site information. Encouraging students to ask hard questions about what they are reading is an important skill in judging the quality of Web site information, and the second step of REAL.

Image Is Not Everything

We sometimes tell children not to judge a book by its cover. Often the same holds true for Web sites. Sites that look important may not be important at all. Sometimes it is difficult to get students to look beyond the colors, pictures, cool Flash animations, and graphics to see what the content is actually saying.

Unlike print material, it's not as clear whether you are reading fiction, nonfiction, editorials, or advertisements on the Web. Therefore, thinking critically about the information on the screen is imperative.

Student Review

Below is a list of guiding questions for students to consider when judging the content of a Web site.

1. Is the information on the Web site useful for your topic?

2. Are additional resources and links provided? Do the links work?

3. Is the site current? Do you know when it was last updated?

4. Do you think the information is accurate?

5. Does the information contradict information you have found elsewhere?

When presenting these questions to students, provide them with a list of Web sites to evaluate and a copy of the "Examine the Content Worksheet" at the end of this chapter. Have students review each site and discuss.

For Students—Evaluating Website Content

Have students evaluate the content of these three sites about frogs. Use the "Examining Content Worksheet" at the end of this chapter to record responses.

The Froggy Page (http://www.frogsonice.com/froggy/)

Frogs (http://www.exploratorium.edu/frogs/index.html)

Froggyville (http://www.froggyville.com/index.php)

> **√ Try This**
>
> Have students search for class resources relating to a particular theme or unit of study. For example, if you are studying a play, such as *Romeo and Juliet*, have them find four or five *Romeo and Juliet* sites. With each site, have students evaluate the content. This is a good way to get them involved in evaluating Web pages while gathering resources for you!

STEP 3. ASK ABOUT THE AUTHOR AND OWNER

Lynn's Story

Martin Luther King, Jr., Day was coming up and I wanted my class to research the civil rights leader in preparation. I asked students to research Martin Luther King, Jr., and the American civil rights movement for homework.

One of my students arrived early the next day with flyers she had downloaded from a Web site. She was eager to show me what she had found. I couldn't believe it. The flyers were basically hate literature about King—my student had no idea.

I asked her which site had the flyers. She told me it was a Martin Luther King site—the address was http://www.martin lutherking.org/. She thought it was a good site because it had his name right in the address and said the flyers were there for students to hand out.

When I went to a computer in the classroom and typed in the same URL, the site was unavailable. It was blocked by our school filter. (I checked it later that night at home. It was obviously a white supremacist site dedicated to defaming the civil rights leader.) I then tried a search in Google on Martin Luther King, just like my student had done at home the night before. Sure enough the site was on the first page of the search results—right near the top.

This whole experience made me really question the role of filters. The majority of my students have access to the Internet outside of school. I figure somehow there needs to be a balance between protecting them through filters and teaching them how to question everything they read.

Anyone who wants to be an author or a publisher on the Web can easily fulfill that dream. It's one of the beauties of the Internet. The drawback, however, is that not all Web site authors are going to be reputable and reliable sources of information. Some sites, such as this Martin Luther King site, are downright insidious.

A key skill to validating Web sites is learning how to check for author and ownership information. Asking about the author and owner is the third step of REAL.

Author's Note

We do not condone sites of this nature; however, the reality is that if a student conducts a search for Martin Luther King in Google, the site used in this example generally appears in the top five results, claiming it is a "valuable resource for students and teachers." Research suggests that students are most likely to choose results on or near the top of a list of results, so many are likely to click on this site.

Ask About the Author

Just as you might teach students not to cite a book without knowing who is responsible for the information, consider applying those same principals to Web pages. Along with recognizing the author of a site, students should also be trying to establish author credibility with respect to a Web site's topic.

For Students

Have students visit a series of Web sites related to a given subject area that you have preselected. Try to find an assortment of sites that supply author information and some that do not. With each site have them answer these questions.

1. Is the author's name provided?
2. Is there a contact person or an address provided?
3. Is there biographical information provided about the author?
4. Does the author seem knowledgeable? Is he or she an expert in the field?
5. What kinds of results do you see when you do a search on the author's name?

If there is no information about the author, students should be careful about wholly trusting the information on the Web page. They may need to validate more.

Student Review—Find the Author

Have students visit the following Web sites. With respect to each, have students answer the questions above.

Lobster Liberation (http://www.lobsterlib.com/index.html)

Feline Reactions to Bearded Men (http://www.improbable.com/airchives/classical/cat/cat.html)

Augustine of Hippo (http://www.georgetown.edu/faculty/jod/)

California Velcro Crop under Challenge (http://home.inreach.com/kumbach/velcro.html)

Who Authored the MartinLutherKing.org Site?

Very often a Web site author will not list his or her name on a site. This seems to be the case with the MartinLutherKing.org site.

Sometimes reading the URL of a site will give you clues about author information, since the domain name of a site may tell you who published or who owns the site. For example, a URL that includes *cnn.com* tells us that the site is owned and published by CNN. We don't know exactly who the author is by looking at the URL, but it may be safe to assume whatever is written was done so by a CNN reporter.

Unfortunately, the URL *http://www.martinlutherking.org/* doesn't tell you much at all. In fact it is rather misleading. The domain name, *martin lutherking.org,* strongly suggests that the site is about Martin Luther King. The extension in the domain name, *.org,* stands for organization. We do know that some extensions are more reliable than others, for example, *.gov* and *.edu* access government and academic sites. The extension *.org* is a tricky one. Many reputable Web sites have *.org* in their URL, but please note this extension is available to anyone.

There is no evidence of a personal page or personal directory, as was the case with Dr. Butz's site. None of the usual clues that would indicate a personal site, such as a tilde or percent sign, the words *users* or *members,* or a personal name is apparent.

Conclusion? After a quick scan, this URL looks like the Web site might contain legitimate information and provide a valuable lesson. First, it includes the name of an important figure. Second, *.org* is an extension used by many organizations that are reputable and provide quality information. Many students might think they had found a great resource just by looking at the URL. How do you know to be wary of a URL that looks innocent enough?

One solution is to validate it further using the easyWhois site and the Wayback Machine.

easyWhois

You may not always be able to find out who wrote a Web site, but sometimes you can find out who owns it. Knowing who owns a Web site is somewhat similar to knowing who publishes a book. Sometimes the owner is the author of a Web site, but not always.

Knowing who owns a Web site is a useful validating tool. Because anyone can be a publisher on the Internet, you want to ensure the author or owner of the site is a qualified and reliable source of information. Unfortunately you cannot rely on the site author to be entirely honest!

√ Try This

To find out who owns the Martin Luther King site, go to easyWhois at http://www.easywhois.com/.

This site is a directory service that collects information from the Internet to track who owns and is responsible for a domain name. Enter the domain of the site you are researching; for example: martinluther king.org. Click next.

Once you scroll through the information you receive, you will find dates the site was created, specific contact names, and addresses at which the organization is based. You will also learn the name of the organization responsible for this site. In this case it's Stormfront, Inc. (Look to registrant information.)

The Martin Luther King Web site is published by an organization called Stormfront. You may have noticed the *.org*. This suggests that *Stormfront.org* may be a Web address on its own. In fact if you type it into a search engine, you will come to the owner's home page, which is a white supremacist site—a site from which you do not want students reading and researching information about civil rights.

Using easyWhois can help you find owner information for almost all Web sites. However, it is possible to bury information about Web site ownership if an owner hires another company to publish a site under the hired name—then it cannot be traced.

Researching Web site owner information may not be something you will want your students to do all the time, but it may be revealing if they are at all concerned about the quality of information on a site and want to know more about it. It is an option of which they should be aware.

For Students

Try this activity with students. Have them go to easyWhois (http://www.easy whois.com/) and find the owner of the site HarryPotter.com.

Tips for Using easyWhois

- Type the domain name of the address you are validating in the search box (remove the *http://* and/or *www.*).
- If you use another address longer than the ones provided, truncate from right to left up to the first forward slash.

For a more advanced Whois report including search engine rank, owner history, and registrar data, try http://www.domaintools.com/. This site also lets you see the traffic report. You can see that for the Martin Luther King site regular traffic is about 20,000 visits per month, except for the month of Martin Luther King Day. During January the traffic jumps to 80,000. Are any of your students part of this statistic?

The Wayback Machine

History buffs take note. One of the great things about the Internet is that it's possible to chart the history of a Web site. In bookstores, we only see the finished product of a body of work, but the Internet allows us to explore a collection of drafts with a validating tool called the Wayback Machine.

√ Try This

To illustrate how the Wayback Machine works, try finding the history of the Martin Luther King site.

Start by visiting the Wayback Machine at http://www.archive.org/. The Wayback Machine (also known as the Internet Archive) is a digital library of Internet sites and other cultural artifacts in digital form. Like a paper library, it provides free access to researchers and the general public.

(Continued)

(Continued)

To use this site, type in the URL of a site or page where you would like to start, and click the Take Me Back button. Once you have conducted a search, select a specific date from the archived dates available. If one particular date does not provide a viewable result, try another. You'll quickly find one that works.

To continue with our example, type *www.martinlutherking.org* in the search box.

The Wayback Machine allows you to browse through 30 billion Web pages archived from 1996 to a few months ago. The first archive of this particular Web site dates from April 21, 1999. Click on one of the links for 1999 and compare the content with today's Web site. You will notice all of the content has changed, text, links, photos. In 1999 there is no reference to schools on the Web site. In 2007 there is a link to download flyers to hand out at your school. It is a very revealing comparison about how this site has moved toward a site aimed at children since its first appearance on the Web.

If you click on the first archive, you will see how the site used to look. While on this page, scroll to the bottom. Note that the heading, *Stormfront.org*, is front and center on the site. When you check other dates, note whether the heading *Stormfront* has been removed from the home page or is clearly visible.

The purpose of looking for the history of a site is to establish whether any changes have been made throughout the years that might shed light on the reliability of information on a particular site. For example, removing the name and the link *Stormfront* from the home page of the MartinLutherKing.org site might be misleading to anyone searching for academic-type information. Checking the history of a site also provides an interesting sense of how the site has evolved, such is the case with the example below for students.

For Students

Try having students search for sites using the Wayback Machine. A good bet is the Harry Potter site, HarryPotter.com. It's seen a lot of changes over the years.

Similar to using easyWhois, researching through the archives of a Web site may not be something students will do very often. But again, it may be revealing if they are at all concerned about the quality of information on a site and want to know more about it. Using the archives is also handy if you are looking for a site that used to be on the Web and is now no longer available.

CONCLUSION

The first three steps of the REAL validating process provide teachers and students with general guidelines and scaffolds for approaching the task of evaluating Web site information. These are building blocks to critical thinking and keeping safe on the Web. Knowing how to read a URL, check the history of a site, or see who owns it are rudimentary skills. If you apply the same principles to print material, you are basically looking for information that would be found in a book jacket. Don't let the Web fool you! Students need to apply the same scrutiny to sources found on the Internet as they would to sources found in the library—or any other media for that matter.

Carolyn's Story

I read an essay by author Amy Tan in her book *The Opposite of Fate*. She writes about how she discovered all this faulty information about her on the Internet, including the fact that she was married to her second husband (she only has had one husband), plus many other errors large and small (that she won a Nobel or Pulitzer, that she had a fight in a public place, and so on). She finally decided to write this essay correcting all of these errors and post it to the Internet in the hopes it would be found in a search as well. Though her essay was amusing and a little satirical as well as serious, it's something that is also very accessible reading to students, especially those familiar with Amy Tan. (See http://www.amytan.net/MythsAndLegends.aspx.)

While I do think students in high school have some skills at discerning the value of the sites they are using, coaching them and getting them to verbalize those skills more, I think, can go a long way toward making them more intellectual users of the Web. And of course it is like being a consumer of any media, from blogs, to TV—can you accept what is presented or do you follow up and verify the information important to you?

RESOURCES

A Short Introduction to the Study of Holocaust Revisionism (http://pubweb.northwestern.edu/~abutz/di/intro.html). *Now can be found by entering the above URL into the Wayback Machine at Archive.org*

Augustine of Hippo (http://www.georgetown.edu/faculty/jod/)

California Velcro Crop under Challenge (http://home.inreach.com/kumbach/velcro.html)

easyWhois (http://www.easywhois.com/)

domaintools (http://www.domaintools.com/)

Feline Reactions to Bearded Men (http://www.improbable.com/airchives/classical/cat/cat.html)

Frogs (http://www.exploratorium.edu/frogs/index.html)

The Froggy page (http://www.frogsonice.com/froggy/)

Froggyville (http://www.froggyville.com/index.php)

Harry Potter (http://www.harrypotter.com/)

Lobster Liberation (http://www.lobsterlib.com/index.html)

Martin Luther King Site (http://www.martinlutherking.org/)

Northwestern Response to Arthur Butz (http://www.ibiblio.org/team/history/controversy/970107-Butz.html)

Wayback Machine (http://www.archive.org/)

E = EXAMINE THE CONTENT WORKSHEET

For each site you visit, answer these questions.

Web site _____

Is the information on the site helpful? Yes/No

Does the site have more resources and links? Do the links work? Yes/No

Is the site up to date? Can I tell when it was last updated? Yes/No

Is the information correct? Yes/No

Are the facts different from information I have found elsewhere? Yes/No

Web site _____

Is the information on the site helpful? Yes/No

Does the site have more resources and links? Do the links work? Yes/No

Is the site up to date? Can I tell when it was last updated? Yes/No

Is the information correct? Yes/No

Are the facts different from information I have found elsewhere? Yes/No

Web site _____

Is the information on the site helpful? Yes/No

Does the site have more resources and links? Do the links work? Yes/No

Is the site up to date? Can I tell when it was last updated? Yes/No

Is the information correct? Yes/No

Are the facts different from information I have found elsewhere? Yes/No

ASSESSMENT

1. Why might I want to know when a site was last updated?
   a. To ensure the information on the site is up to date—especially if I am researching time-sensitive materials.
   b. If the site hasn't been updated for many years, it may mean that the Webmaster has abandoned the site.
   c. Depending on my topic, it may not matter about when the last update was.
   d. All of the above.

2. Which of the following is NOT a question to ask when examining the content of a Web site?
   a. Is the information on the Web site useful for my topic?
   b. Are additional resources and links provided?
   c. Are there movie features provided?
   d. Do the links work?

3. In what ways does knowing the owner of a Web site offer clues about a Web site's purpose?
   a. The owner may be affiliated with a group that has a specific agenda.
   b. The owner's address can provide clues.
   c. The owner of a Web site will tell you about his or her purpose.
   d. The owner may try to provide incorrect owner information.

4. What are some instances in which you might use the Wayback Machine to validate Internet information?
   a. To see if you can find a Web site that you can't seem to access anymore.
   b. To see if a Web author has changed the site to try and submerge a particular bias.
   c. To find out more information about a site, in general.
   d. All of the above.

5. A Web site that has *.org* in its Web address can be owned by anybody. True or false?

6. Which of the following is NOT an "Ask About the Author" question?
   a. Does the author seem knowledgeable?
   b. Is the name of the publisher provided?
   c. Is there a contact person or an address provided?
   d. Is there biographical information provided about the author?
   e. Is he or she an expert in the field?

7. What makes the example of the MartinLutherKing.org Web address particularly alarming?

a. It contains the name Martin Luther King right in the URL, which makes the site seem legitimate.

b. Many sites that contain *.org* are reputable and provide great information—this one is an exception.

c. This site appears on the first page of a list of Google search results when one conducts a search for *"Martin Luther King"*.

d. All of the above.

8. The Web site easyWhois is a good validating tool because it allows you to research the _____ of a Web site.

a. Owner

b. Validator

c. Writer

d. Brander

Answer Key: 1. d; 2. c; 3. a; 4. d; 5. True; 6. b; 7. d; 8. a

QUESTIONS FOR EXTENDED THOUGHT AND DISCUSSION

1. How can bogus Web sites be useful in preparing students to engage with the Internet?

2. What are the comparisons between the grammar and syntax of print with the Web?

3. Similar to Amy Tan who discovered that there are many versions of the truth about her own life on the Web, what would you do if you discovered old pictures and inaccurate information about your own important personal experiences?

Look at the Links

Kevin's Story

I'm a fourth grade teacher who uses the Save the Pacific Northwest Tree Octopus site regularly. The first time I ever showed my class they were skeptical, but due to the power of persuasion and authoritative looking site, they believed the tree octopus did exist.

We analyzed the site in detail and I asked them to apply some common sense. Many caught on immediately, but there were others who believed the creature was real. I thought we could look it up in Google to prove once and for all the creature did not exist. To my horror, thousand of sites appeared referring and linking to the same site. I tried to be rational and offered to look it up in the encyclopedia, but several students piped up that it wouldn't be there because this octopus was a subspecies and not all animals could be listed in the encyclopedia!

Students left my class debating whether the creature was real. At the time, I really wish I would have known a trick or two to prove to them it was definitively a hoax.

In the previous chapter, we have already considered some options Kevin might use to validate the information on the tree octopus site. In this chapter we focus on a few more. The fourth step of REAL is look at the links. There are basically two types of links, forward links and back links.

FORWARD LINKS AND BACK LINKS

A forward link is the name given to a link from your Web site to a page on someone else's Web site. A back link is the name given to a link from someone else's Web site to a page on your Web site.

The URL of the link is imbedded in the site, meaning that if you click on the highlighted text or button referring to the link, you retrieve the outside URL and move to that site. Because you leave the original Web site and move to another, a new URL appears in your browser's address bar.

Investigating forward links of Web sites can be an important validating step because it can sometimes help students evaluate whether a site contains biased, false, or quality information.

Link Tip

To quickly check the URLs of forward links, move your cursor over a piece of linked text or graphic. The arrow turns into a hand and a URL appears in the status bar at the lower left of your browser. That's a quick trick to show students how to scan URLs of forward links quickly.

Student Review

When looking at forward links use these guiding questions:

Question 1: What are the URLs of the forward links?

The reason for checking the URL of a forward link is straightforward. It can help you to see any patterns of reference. For example, I would become concerned if every single forward link contained the same domain name as the home page. If I am reading what is supposed to be an academic source, I am looking for a range of forward links that take me to universities, museums, or government research sites. Of course, as with any single strategy of validation, this approach can backfire. It would be possible for any Web site to try to gain credibility by inserting forward links to an academic site.

Question 2: Do the domain names change?

Chance of bias in information increases in an academic-type Web site if the same person writes all of the referenced material. Think of the equivalent in print material. If one author writes a book and all of the referenced sources within it, you probably wouldn't consider it to be quality research. Therefore, it is important to look at the URLs of forward links to see who has written them. If the same domain name appears again and again in the forward links, and does not change, this pattern might suggest bias.

For Students—Analyzing the Save the Pacific Northwest Tree Octopus Site

The Save the Pacific Northwest Tree Octopus site is a good site to use when teaching students about links. Not only is the site beautifully presented and quite persuasive, it has great links to other sites you might want to use in the classroom.

In this activity, have students analyze several of the forward links of the site with respect to the three guiding questions above.

Have students go to http://zapatopi.net/treeoctopus/ and choose several forward links. They will appear in green highlighted text, both in the text of the page and on the side menu. After students answer the guiding questions for each, have them answer these summary questions: Are there any links on this site to trustworthy sources that prove that the tree octopus exists? What are they? What makes these sites trustworthy in your eyes?

Back to Zack

Reflecting back on Zack's story in the previous chapter, if he had checked the forward links on the Short Introduction to the Study of Holocaust Revisionism site, he might have disregarded the information straight away. Every single link on the page contained the same domain name. Arthur Butz is the sole source of all of his links.

Susan's Story

I was teaching middle school social studies in Ontario at the time. The mother of one of my top students requested a meeting with me after school. His mom had found out that her 14-year-old had built his own Web site and was pretending to be a lawyer offering free legal advice.

On the Web site, her son had invented an impressive set of credentials and degrees from Harvard and Stanford. She was astonished to find out that individuals from around the world—twice his age—were actually writing him asking for advice, and he was answering them. She wanted to know what I thought about what she should do—aside from write to the people and tell them they were getting advice from a 14-year-old . . .

Clearly, her son needed to learn how serious it is to pretend to be an expert and offer advice to unsuspecting people. He needed to learn the ethics and social responsibility of having anonymous power to pretend to be anyone at his fingertips. A good assignment for her son would be to write a code of ethics for online behavior to be reviewed by his school.

It's possible for a child to build an authentic-looking site, invent imaginary names and credentials, plus create forward links to some truly authentic sites, such as the Harvard Law School. What Web authors cannot control, however, is who links to their site. Checking to see who has linked to a site or examining the back links can be revealing. It's phase two of the fourth step of REAL.

What Is a Back Link?

Back links are like digital threads that come from other sites. Any author can choose to link to another site—an author may even create a link to his or her own work. Back links are invisible. Unlike forward links, which are controlled by a Web site author, anyone in the world can create a link to a site from an external source. There are no link police!

Why Examine Back Links?

A quick look to see who has linked to a site gives you perspective about the quality of information. A list of external links potentially provides a range of thoughts or comments about any given page. In the case of the 14-year-old "lawyer", chances are the links to his site were few in number (if there were any at all) and it's probably safe to say that none of the links were from sites in the academic or legal field. More likely they were links from the boy's friends.

The reasons why someone chooses to link to another site vary, but usually some sort of purpose exists. Establishing who has linked to another site and what that purpose might be can help validate Internet information.

Student Review

When searching for back links, ask three guiding questions:

Question 1: Who is linked to the Web site?

Look to see what other groups or individuals have linked to it. Are they schools or commercial sites? Read the URLs and titles carefully. Are there any patterns in the types of sites?

Question 2: Why are they linked?

What is the purpose of the link? Why have groups or individuals chosen to create a link to this site?

Question 3: What do other sites say about the material on the site?

Gain perspective about a site by reading what another site tells you about it. Cross-reference information and look for hidden bias.

Different search sites offer varying methods for creating a list of back links. The one I generally use involves the use of the AltaVista search engine, along with the link: command.

√ Try This

Here's an example of how to generate a list of back links. This example uses a bogus Web site dedicated to showing the harmful effects of dihydrogen monoxide (otherwise known as water!). The site address is http://www.dhmo.org/.

1. Go to AltaVista (http://www.altavista.com/).

2. In the search box type *link:http://www.dhmo.org/*. Be sure to leave no space before or after the colon.

3. Once you click the Find button, you will see an assortment of sites that have chosen to link to this site. Remember the questions to ask.

4. Can you make any generalizations about this site? What perspectives do you gain after looking at the back links?

For Students

Have students try to find the back links to the following sites. First have them visit the site. Once they've reviewed it, get them to go to AltaVista and follow the steps outlined in the Back Link Tips found at the end of this chapter.

Once students find a list of back links, have them respond to these three questions.

1. Who is linked to the Web site?

2. Why are they linked?

3. What do other sites say about the material on the site?

Sites to Use

California's Velcro Crop under Challenge (http://home.inreach.com/kumbach/velcro.html)

Feline Reactions to Bearded Men (http://www.improbable.com/airchives/classical/cat/cat.html)

Genochoice (http://www.genochoice.com/)

Link: Command Tip

If you are researching a URL and produce zero results, try truncating the address. Truncating can also help if the URL you are researching is long. To truncate, delete one folder at a time, moving from right to left. Each time delete to the previous left slash (/).

Who Is Linked to Your School?

You might be interested in knowing who is linked to your school Web site. It is not a bad idea to run a periodic check on the back links to your school. (If you have your own class Web site, you might want to check that as well.)

I recently met a school leader who had checked for back links on his school's site. The principal found that someone had linked a site to the school's and was publishing some very unpleasant things about the school and various staff members. By researching the owner of the site, the principal managed to deal with the situation. At this particular school, leaders now regularly check back links on their school's and all of their and teachers' sites.

On another occasion I met with a group of school leaders whose Web site was getting e-mail from all over the world. Notes would arrive from various countries requesting more materials on school leadership. The group wondered why they were getting so much e-mail. After running a back link check, they discovered that the United Nations had linked to their site. The United Nations had cited it as an example of exemplary material and lots of other schools had made links to it as a result. You can imagine how thrilled they were.

√ Try This

Investigate the back links of your school's Web site. In AltaVista start with *link:* in the search box, then type in your school URL. Remember to leave no space before or after the colon.

Advanced Commands

Sometimes when you generate a list of back links, the list is so long that it is impossible to sort through the results. There may be instances when you want more specific information. For example, perhaps you want to know how many education sites have linked to a specific Web site. Perhaps you are interested in seeing how other educators are using the material.

To target a list of back links, you need to use a special search, called the host: command, along with the link: command. The host: command allows you to search through Web pages hosted by certain groups or categories, such as schools, universities, and companies. All you need to do is add *host:* to the search, plus one specific extension, such as *.edu* or *.ac.uk.*

√ Try This

For this example, we will generate a list of all higher education sites that have links to the Martin Luther King site.

To tackle this, we first need to generate a list of back links from the Martin Luther King Web site.

1. Go to AltaVista, and in the search box type *link:www.martin lutherking.org* in the search box.

2. Add *host:edu* to the search so it looks like this: *link:www.martin lutherking.org + host:edu.*

3. With this search, the number of results should decrease and you should have a list of higher education sites that have links. Look to see the extension *.edu* in the URL of each result.

This purpose of this list from a validating point of view is to provide you with some perspective as to what higher education authors think about the Martin Luther King site.

Tips for Using the Host: Command

You can add *host:* with an extension to the link: command. Just be sure of the following:

- Only search for one extension at a time.
- Use the plus sign or leave a space when adding the host: command.
- There should be no space after either colon.

CONCLUSION

Although implementing each step of REAL on its own may not be an entirely foolproof way of validating information, one or two of them combined may help you and students get definitive answers about the endangered tree octopus or whether to trust the "lawyer" offering free advice! These are building blocks to critical thinking and keeping safe on the Web

The importance of giving students these evaluative skills and tools cannot be overemphasized—especially since many may be working at home, in unfiltered environments. Sites such as the MartinLutherKing.org site and the Butz Holocaust revisionism site clearly demonstrate the need for teaching children about Web site awareness. It is an important part of a child's education—it is also an important part of keeping them safe.

BACK LINK TIPS

The link: command allows you to create a list of back links. It is an excellent validating tool if you are unsure about the quality of information on a Web site.

How Do I Start?

1. Go to AltaVista, and in the search box, type *link:*.

2. Leaving no space after the colon, type the address of the Web site you are researching. For example, to find the back links to the site Feline Reactions to Bearded Men, type the following in the search box: *link:http://www.improbable.com/airchives/classical/cat/cat.html*

3. Click the Find button and you will find an assortment of sites.

0 Results?

If you are researching a URL and produce no results, try truncating the URL. To truncate, delete one folder at a time, moving from right to left. Each time delete to the previous slash.

Removing */airchives/classical/cat/cat.html* from the Feline Reaction to Bearded Men search mentioned above will provide a longer list of results.

RESOURCES

A Short Introduction to the Study of Holocaust Revisionism (http://pubweb.northwestern.edu/~abutz/di/intro.html). *Now can be found by entering the above URL into the Wayback Machine at Archive.org.*

AltaVista (http://www.altavista.com/)

California Velcro Crop under Challenge (http://home.inreach.com/kumbach/velcro.html)

Dihydrogen Monoxide (http://www.dhmo.org/)

Feline Reactions to Bearded Men (http://www.improbable.com/airchives/classical/cat/cat.html)

Genochoice (http://www.genochoice.com/)

Martin Luther King Site (http://www.martinlutherking.org/)

The Pacific Northwest Tree Octopus (http://zapatopi.net/tree octopus/)

Wayback Machine (http://www.archive.org/)

ASSESSMENT

1. What did you learn by examining a few of the forward links on the Pacific Northwest Tree Octopus Web site?
   a. The octopus is a real creature.
   b. None of the links was convincing—none proved the existence of the octopus.
   c. The links were all authentic.
   d. All links were probably written by the same author.

2. What would be the results in Altavista.com if you were to type *link:www.martinlutherking.org link: www.stormfront.org host:edu* and search?
   a. Pages from higher education with links to http://www.martin lutherking.org/
   b. Pages from higher education with links in to http://www .stormfront.org/
   c. Pages from higher education with links to http://www.martin lutherking.org/ and http://www.stormfront.org/

3. You can often recognize a personal Web site by looking for a _____ in the URL.
   a. *
   b. ~
   c. %
   d. #
   e. Both b and d
   f. Both b and c

4. A quick way to check the URLs of forward links on a site is to place your cursor over the link and read the URL in bottom left corner of your screen. True or false?

5. What can you infer if the domain name of a forward link is the same as the main site?
   a. The two sites are probably unrelated.
   b. It tells you nothing.
   c. The information on the forward link is probably written by the same author.
   d. None of the above.

6. Which of the following is NOT a question to ask when looking at the forward links of a site?
   a. What are the URLs of the forward links?
   b. Do the domain names change?
   c. Is the information biased?
   d. Do the links work?

7. A pattern of forward links that shows the author continually referencing his or her own materials should make the reader question the information. True or false?

8. Mapping incoming links to a Web site can be valuable because:
   a. You can see who has been given permission by the author of the Web page to link to the Web site.
   b. You can see how other sites are referencing the Web page who do not have the author's permission.
   c. You can see the reference sources the author used for his or her own content.

9. How does analyzing a Web site's back links help validate Internet information?
   a. It helps establish how quickly a link can take us to another site.
   b. It shows more information about what's on a Web page.

    c. It gives us more URLs to research.

    d. It provides us with important cross-reference information.

10. If I am adding a host: command search to the link: command in AltaVista, I should:

    a. Leave no space after the colon.

    b. Use the plus sign or leave a space on either side of the word or phrase.

    c. Put quotation marks around phrases.

    d. All of the above.

Answer Key: 1. b; 2. c; 3. f; 4. True; 5. c; 6. d; 7. True; 8. b; 9. d; 10. d

QUESTIONS FOR EXTENDED THOUGHT AND DISCUSSION

1. Run a search on the links coming into your school site. Are there any patterns in those links?

2. Did you find student sites, real estate sites, or university sites?

3. How would you respond to the student who pretended to be an online lawyer?

4. How would you integrate these skills across the curriculum?

Research Outside the Box

A Guide to Smart Searching

Kate's Story

At a recent conference in England, Kate approached me to talk about a friend who had just been diagnosed with multiple sclerosis (MS). When the doctor was explaining MS to Kate's friend, he cautioned about researching information on the Internet. He strongly suggested that she not use the Internet as an information source.

When I heard this, I immediately speculated that the doctor was concerned about the patient finding misleading information. Kate agreed and said that the doctor was worried about her finding an instant cure and giving her false hope.

Together we typed *"multiple sclerosis"* into a search engine. The doctor's fears were confirmed. Near the top of the results list was a Web site that promised an 80 percent cure.

At some point in your life, either you or someone you know may very well be faced with a situation like Kate's. While unpleasant to think about, these are the very situations that make the ability to validate Web information so critical. Understanding validation as well as effective search techniques will help you both lessen the number of dubious sites that you might find and evaluate the ones that remain. Good search skills on the Web can be an ounce of prevention against finding junk on the Web.

By junk, I mean misleading information about medical issues, pornography, hate sites—the list goes on. As you've probably experienced, sometimes the most harmless of searches can unearth sites you may not care to read.

This chapter is dedicated to "out of the box" research—search techniques that move beyond using search engines in typical ways. Through the next sections you will learn how to add extensions, country codes, and virtual indexes to your searching repertoire. These shortcuts allow you to target your searches for specific topics, plus connect you to teacher Web sites or resources from around the world.

SEARCH WITH EXTENSIONS

A brief refresher about extensions: They are bits of information found in a Web site's domain name and refer to groups or categories. For example, in the URL http://www.thebritishmuseum.ac.uk/compass/, the domain name is *thebritishmuseum.ac.uk*. The extensions are *.ac* and *.uk*. (*.ac* stands for academic institution, commonly used outside of the United States; *.uk* stands for the United Kingdom.)

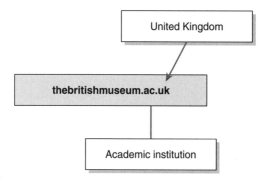

A few other examples of extensions are *.k12, .gov, .edu,* and *.com.*

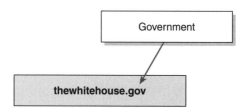

Extensions can be used in a search to help pinpoint specific categories. For instance, Kate's friend might be better off searching for information about multiple sclerosis from sites published by the government. (A search like this would target sites that have the characters *.gov* in their domain name.)

Here's the rationale. Most hospitals and reputable health organizations have the extension *.org* in their domain name (e.g. childrenshospital .org and cancercare.org). The problem with .org domains is that anyone in the world can purchase them, and therefore, you cannot assume that all .org sites are going to be trustworthy sources of information (remember MartinLutherKing.org?). One of the best first-round search strategies for Kate is to limit her results to sites that are not trying to sell her a cure. Only government agencies can purchase and use *.gov* in their domain names. This particular extension is closed to the general public. Therefore, searching within .gov sites guarantees your results will be limited to Web addresses that have a .gov extension. In other words, a search that only looks through Web sites that have the extension *.gov* in the domain name provides a *closed* search environment.

√ Try This

A surefire way to search with extensions is to use the host: command search in AltaVista. You start by going to http://www.altavista.com/ and typing *host:* in the search box, followed by your keyword or keyword phrase. An example might be: *host:gov + "multiple sclerosis"*.

| host:gov + "multiple sclerosis" | FIND |

Search Tip

Always put keyword phrases in quotation marks to ensure the words appear together exactly as you have entered them. Use the plus sign to join words or phrases. Including or excluding the dot before *gov* will not affect results.

Note that when you try this search, all the URLs in your list of results (they will be in green) include the extension *.gov*. When I recently did this search, the first Web site was http://www.nlm.nih.gov/medlineplus/multiplesclerosis.html. This is a site sponsored by the National Library of Medicine and the National Institutes of Health.

For Students

Students are probably familiar with seeing extensions such as *.com, .gov,* and *.org* in Web addresses. But are they familiar with what all extensions represent? Using the Extension Guide at the end of this chapter, what might you know about a site that contains the following extensions?

Example: .co.jp = a company in Japan

1. .gov.au =
2. .ac.nz =
3. .sch.uk =

Suggested Responses:

1. .gov.au = This site will be from the Australian government.
2. .ac.nz = This site will be from an academic institution in New Zealand.
3. .sch.uk = This site will be from a school in the United Kingdom.

Digging for Gold—Extensions in Student Research

Involving extensions as a search technique can lead to fascinating resources, targeted information, and improved critical thinking. The goal is to get students to think creatively about the searches they are conducting and to make the most of the host: command and extensions.

√ Try This

For example, if a student needed resources to access the current population or immigration statistics in the United States, instead of plugging the subject *statistics* or *population* into a search engine and accessing over 13 million results, a host: command search in AltaVista that looks like *host:gov + statistics* is much more specific.

In this search you are searching for all pages indexed under government Web sites that contain the word *statistics.*

If you were looking for specific statistics, such as the population of the state of Arizona, you could add the words *population* and *arizona* to the search so it looks like this: *host:gov + statistics + population + arizona.*

The possibilities are endless, given the number of topics a student might research, the extensions he or she might use, and the countries within which he or she might search.

For Students

In this activity, students play a guessing game whereby they generate a "best guess" of a host: command search given the suggested topic. Invent a possible search request that uses common extensions and country codes. You will need to refer to the Extension Guide at the end of this section. Assume that all of the searches will be done in AltaVista. Follow these tips.

Search Tips

- Be sure to type in the AltaVista search box, not the address bar.
- Leave no space before or after the colon.
- Use the plus sign when adding words.
- Leave a space on either side of the plus sign.
- Put phrases in quotation marks.

Example

Scenario: You are researching population statistics in the United Kingdom.
Search: host:gov.uk + population

Scenarios

1. Scenario: You are researching universities in Japan.
   Search: host: _____

2. Scenario: You are researching school sites in the United Kingdom that include the word *poetry*.
   Search: host: _____

3. Scenario: You are researching cancer research in U.S. government sites.
   Search: host: _____

4. Scenario: You are researching weather patterns in New Zealand.
   Search: host: _____

5. Scenario: You are researching birth rates in Ethiopia.
   Search: host: _____

6. Scenario: You are researching football scores in the United Kingdom.
   Search: host: _____

Have students test their searches to see if they solicit good results.

Suggested Responses

1. You are researching universities in Japan: host:jp + .ac.

2. You are researching school sites in the United Kingdom that include the word *poetry*: host:uk + .sch + poetry.

(Continued)

(Continued)

3. You are researching cancer research in government sites: host:gov + "cancer research".

4. You are researching weather patterns in New Zealand: host:nz + "weather pattern".

5. You are researching birth rates in Ethiopia: host:et + "birth rate" + .gov.

6. You are researching football scores in the United Kingdom: host:uk + "football scores".

CREATING A VIRTUAL INDEX

Mark's Story

I often hear other teachers talk about great resources they've found on the Web. I've tried searching through some of the sites they suggest—Education World, CNN, DiscoverySchool, NASA—and I do find interesting materials, but I have to admit it's very time consuming and overwhelming with all the links that go off in a million directions. Often I find really good stuff I'd like to use, but then can't find it again the next time I go back to look.

Tracking down specific content from a large Web site can sometimes be an exercise in frustration. On a large site, with hundreds, or even tens of thousands of pages, it is easy to get lost, overwhelmed, and downright tired of looking. To prevent all of the above, there is a special search feature that can allow you to save time when searching for valuable information within large sites. It's called creating a virtual index or a quick list of Web pages with the same root domain name.

Earth to Mars

To illustrate how the virtual index works, try creating one with the NASA Web site. NASA's site is an example of a large site that houses millions of Web pages in a variety of subject areas (it includes great teaching materials and student activities). To create an index, use the host: command search in AltaVista. This is the same command used with extensions. In this case, however, we are using it to search for results from one full domain name, nasa.gov.

√ Try This

Go to AltaVista and in the search box type: *host:nasa.gov*. Please only type the domain name, leave out *www.* and *http://*. You should retrieve a long list of pages from the NASA site. The actual number of nasa.gov pages will be displayed at the top of your search. If you look at the URL of each (the green line of each result), you will see they all include *nasa.gov* in the URL. Please note that there are no sponsored sites at the top.

This list represents an index of the site, similar to the index in the back of a book. However, the list is neither alphabetized nor arranged by category. With a few commands you can organize it to suit your needs. It's possible to pinpoint particular pages or resources by adding specific words or phrases to this query.

Refine Your Index

Try narrowing your search by adding a phrase or a keyword. For example, *host:nasa.gov + mars*.

Your search results should include all the Web pages from this site that include the word *Mars*. If you are interested in any student activities that deal with Mars you could try *host:nasa.gov + mars + "student activities"*.

As the list of links becomes more focused and manageable, you can keep adding, for example, *host:nasa.gov + mars + "sixth grade"*.

Even if you will never use the NASA site in your classroom, the important thing to note is that navigating through a large site is much more manageable and time effective when using the host: command. Just remember when adding words and phrases follow these tips.

Search Tips

- Be sure to type in the AltaVista search box, not the address bar.
- Leave no space before or after the colon.
- Use the plus sign when adding words.
- Leave a space on either side of the plus sign.
- Put phrases in quotation marks.

√ Try This

Create a virtual index for the National Geographic site. Your initial search in AltaVista should look like this: *host:nationalgeographic.com*.

In the National Geographic site, you can conduct specific searches for maps, information about geographic areas, animals, and so on. This is a rich resource to use with students.

For Students

Consider putting students into groups and assigning each group a separate geographic area. Have them search for maps, vegetation, or animal life in their area. They can learn about the world and hone search techniques at the same time.

FINDING RESOURCES IN TEACHER WEB SITES

Paul's Story

I was pleasantly surprised one day when one of my seventh graders showed me a site on the Internet that contained a lesson plan relating to a novel we were studying in class. The student wanted to know if he could work on some of the projects listed on the site. Talk about a wake-up call! I instantly wondered why I hadn't thought about tapping into other teachers' ideas for research projects and lesson plans—and why wasn't I getting my students involved in the process? I was fascinated that my student wanted to tackle an assignment from another teacher's Web site.

Some wonderful teaching resources are available on the Web. Lesson plans often have useful links to museums, photo galleries, primary documents, and projects perfect for providing a variety of resources and targeting a variety of learning styles. The problem is that so many are available that it's hard to know where to begin.

√ Try This

1. Start by selecting an educational site that houses lesson plans. You may already have a favorite in mind or you might wish to try to search for primary documents in the U.K. or U.S. National Archives. Here are some suggestions:

   DiscoverySchool (http://school.discovery.com/)

   Education World (http://www.education-world.com/)

   WebQuests (http://webquest.org/) or WebQuestUK (http://www.webquestuk.org.uk/)

   U.K. National Archives (http://www.nationalarchives.gov.uk/)

   U.S. National Archives (http://www.archives.gov/)

   Your state, provincial, or national educational department likely will also have a lesson plan bank.

Whichever site you choose, you will use only the domain name when you search (i.e., remove the *http://* and the *www.*).

2. Go to AltaVista and type *host:* plus the domain name of your selected site. For example, *host:school.discovery.com.*

3. After you have completed this basic search, try to target it more to your needs, such as adding a subject area appropriate for the level of your students. For example, a search for activities or lesson plans that discuss global warming would look like this: *host:school .discovery.com + "global warming".*

A search in the U.S. National Archives for Martin Luther King, Jr., might look like this: *host:archives.gov + "martin luther king".*

Here are some other examples:

> host:webquest.org + "specified topic"
>
> host:educationworld.com + "lesson plans" + poetry
>
> host:nationalarchives.gov.uk + churchill

Try adding the titles of specific novels, authors, historic figures, assessment ideas—anything!

For step-by-step instructions for working with the host: command in AltaVista, see the host: command tips at the end of this chapter.

For Students

As Paul suggests, have your students try these searches to find resources for you. This is an interesting way for them to explore projects or assignments in a particular subject area that are of interest to them.

CALLING ALL COLLEAGUES

Jan's Story

I've been an elementary school teacher for two years, and since I'm relatively "new" to this, I'm eager to collect as many lesson plans and teacher resources as possible. Right now I'm in the middle of planning a unit on turtles.

I know I should be able to find lots of interesting information on the Internet, but when I try to do a search with the word turtles I get well over a million results, most of which I don't need. I do not want to buy turtles, or know about chocolate turtles, or the band called the Turtles. I just want to know if there is another teacher out there who has already done class projects and has materials available. How do I do that?

Haiku sites from Japan, mythology sites from Greece, turtle sites from Florida, geography sites from teachers in your own state—it's possible to invite the world and colleagues into your classroom and reach beyond classroom walls for quality resource materials.

Jan might consider two methods of searching to target the information she needs. One method uses AltaVista's host: command with extensions and country codes; the other method uses the url: command. Either of these commands would help her find Web sites from schools that have information or projects dealing with turtles (or any other topic for that matter).

Turtles and the Host: Command

In the beginning of this chapter, we introduced how to search for information using extensions. Now, we basically are doing the same thing, but with a slight variation. To find Web sites from schools that have information about turtles, the extension used is .k12. You also need to add a state code, plus the .us country code. (Please note that not all U.S. schools use the extension .k12—there is no surefire way to access all the schools in the country.)

√ Try This

To find teacher sites about turtles in the state of Florida, go to AltaVista and try this search: *host:k12.fl.us + turtle.*

Note that as you look at your list of results, the green URL in each result includes *k12.fl.us.* You should end up with a long list of sites from across the state of Florida.

Tip

U.S. state codes are the same as U.S. postal codes. When using *.k12* with a particular state, select the state code and add *.us.* For example: *k12.tx.us.*

√ Try This

Try searching for a keyword specific to your curriculum and state. An example search for school sites in Washington would include *.k12.wa.us.* For example: *host:k12.wa.us + salmon.*

Consider investigating topics such as volcanoes in Hawaii, grizzlies in Alaska, the gold rush in California, dolphins in Florida, penguins, global warming, and fossils.

Note: The host: command works wonderfully with certain extensions, but can be tricky for U.S. school sites if you are not sure of the state within which you would like to search. You may not want to access a specific state; you may wish to access sites from the entire country. To do so use the url: command.

Turtles and the Url: Command

The url: command differs slightly from the host: command. The host: command searches for extensions only, and in some cases, as in the case with .k12, it requires the entire extension, such as U.S. state information and .us country code.

The url: command is not as specific. It tries to match the information you type in after the colon and limits your search to Web addresses that contain the same text. For example, if you do a url: command using the letters *edu* (the extension for higher learning in the United States), the search will access all U.S. higher learning sites but it will also access any URL that has the word *education* or *educator* somewhere in its Web address.

If you do the search *url:k12 + turtle*, you will find all sites that have the words *.k12* in the URL and *turtle* somewhere in the site.

√ Try This

Try a search using the url: command in AltaVista by typing in *url:k12 + turtle* (or insert a keyword particular to your subject area).

Search Tip

The key difference between using the host: command and the url: command is the following:

- The host: command searches for extensions only.
- The url: command searches for whatever you type after the colon, only within Web addresses that contain the same text.

If you are unsure of which state to search in, try using the url: command when looking for .k12 sites. If you are looking through .ac sites, .sch sites, or .edu sites, use the host: command.

Take Your Search Global With Country Codes

If you wish to take your search for teacher resources global, you can do that by adding country codes to your search request. To find out what resources there are in South Africa on apartheid or what Japanese sites have resources on haiku poetry, simply add a keyword and a country code to a host: command search. The country code for South Africa is *.za* and the code for Japan is *.jp.*

Refer to the Extension Guide at the end of this chapter for help. For a complete list of country codes refer to http://goes.gsfc.nasa.gov/text/web_country_codes.html.

You can pick and choose which country codes to match with education-specific extensions. Recall that searches with *.k12* and *.edu* will access U.S. sites. (You may be more likely to access teacher Web sites if you add these, but they will be U.S. based.)

The rest of the world does not necessarily follow our structure for organizing Web addresses. For example, the United Kingdom does not use *.k12* for their school sites. Instead they use *.sch* for school and *.ac* for higher academic institutions. They also have a *.uk* in the extension position. For example, the domain name for Oxford is ox.ac.uk.

I have learned that it can be highly motivating for students to use sites from around the world, especially if there are opposing points of view. For example, if you are teaching the American Revolution, you may want to search U.K. academic sites to see if they might have a different point of view. That search would be *host:ac.uk + "American Revolution"*.

√ Try This

Here are some more example challenges to start your global searching. Feel free to use your own keywords and country codes.

Example 1: Apartheid sites in South Africa
   Begin by looking for information about apartheid in sites from South Africa. In AltaVista, try *host:za + apartheid*.

Example 2: Monsoons in India
   Try *host:in + monsoon*.

Example 3: Haiku in Japan
   In the search box type *host:jp + haiku* or *host:ac.jp + haiku*.

   Feel free to design your own global search. Pick a topic and a country code. Start in AltaVista and type *host:* in the search box. Use the sample searches as your guide.

CONCLUSION

Learning how to use all the search techniques covered in this chapter is part and parcel of taking ownership of the grammar of the Internet. These skills encourage you to work with domain names and extensions, and build bridges through large Web sites. Your students will be impressed! There are no guarantees with these "out of the box" type searches; however, thinking creatively and critically about them and the use of country codes can lead to some fascinating resource material for your students and curriculum. It will also help students learn more about how the Web is organized. It is not only about validating information; it's about finding quality resources that are "safe" and bypassing unwanted materials on the Web.

RESOURCES

AltaVista (http://www.altavista.com/)

NASA (http://www.nasa.gov/)

National Geographic (http://www.nationalgeographic.com/)

DiscoverySchool (http://school.discovery.com/)

U.K. National Archives (http://www.nationalarchives.gov.uk/)

U.S. National Archives (http://www.archives.gov/)

Education World (http://www.educationworld.com/)

WebQuests (http://www.webquest.org/)

U.K. WebQuests (http://www.webquestuk.org.uk/)

Postal Code Abbreviations (http://www.50states.com/tools/postal.htm)

Web Country Codes (http://goes.gsfc.nasa.gov/text/web_country_codes.html)

HOST: COMMAND TIPS

The host: command allows you to create a virtual index of all the pages on a given Web site. It is an excellent search tool if you are searching for specific types of sites or if you are navigating through a large one with hundreds of pages.

How Do I Start?

- Go to AltaVista at http://www.altavista.com/. In the search box, type *host:*.
- Leaving no space after the colon, type the address of the site through which you would like to search. Remove the *http://* or *www.* so you are only searching the domain name. For example, to search through the NASA site (http://www.nasa.gov/), the search would be *host:nasa.gov*.
- You should see a list of pages from the site. Have a look at the domain names in the URLs of the results (the green line in each result). They should all contain the domain name.

Want to add more words or phrases? You can. Just remember:

- Use a plus sign or leave a space on either side of each word.
- Put phrases in quotation marks.

An example search that uses words and phrases might look like this: *host:nasa.gov + "student activities"*.

EXTENSION GUIDE

Here are a few of many common extensions.

.edu	Higher education (most U.S. colleges)
.k12	U.S. school site (not all U.S. schools use this)
.sch	Schools in the United Kingdom (not all U.K. schools use this)
.ac	Academic institution (outside of U.S.)
.com	Commercial
.co	Company (usually used with a country code: e.g., co.uk)
.org	Any organization
.gov	Government agency
.net	Network
.mil	U.S. military

COUNTRY CODES

Here are some examples of country codes.

.at	Austria	.ie	Ireland
.au	Australia	.in	India
.ca	Canada	.iq	Iraq
.ch	Switzerland	.it	Italy
.cn	China	.jp	Japan
.de	Germany	.nz	New Zealand
.es	Spain	.pk	Pakistan
.et	Ethiopia	.uk	United Kingdom
.fr	France	.us	United States
.gr	Greece	.za	South Africa

ASSESSMENT

1. Match the word on the left to the appropriate extension on the right.

1.	Higher learning	a.	.net
2.	Commercial	b.	.ac
3.	Network	c.	.edu
4.	U.K. school	d.	.org
5.	Organization	e.	.com
6.	Government	f.	.gov
7.	Academic institution	g.	.co.uk
8.	U.K. company	h.	.sch

2. Anyone that wants to have a .gov Web site may have one. True or false?

3. What is the purpose of using the host: command? Why is it an efficient search tool?
   a. The host: command allows you to create a virtual index.
   b. The host: command allows you to pinpoint your search in a large Web site.
   c. The host: command allows you to add words and phrases to your search to make your search even more specific.
   d. All of the above.

4. To create a virtual index in AltaVista for the NASA Web site, the search query should look like:
   a. host: nasa.gov
   b. host:nasa.gov
   c. host:www.nasa.gov
   d. host: + nasa.gov

5. Creating a virtual index is a skill I can apply to any large Web site, as long as I know the URL of the site I am researching. True or false?

6. Which of the following is NOT a consideration when adding words and phrases to the host: command search?
   a. Remove *www.* and *http://* from the URL of the Web site you are researching.
   b. Put phrases in quotation marks.
   c. Leave no spaces in between each keyword you add.
   d. Conduct your search in AltaVista.

7. It's possible to create a virtual index of a large Web site, such as Education World, in AltaVista by using the forward: command. True or false?

8. Creating a virtual index means you are making a list of all the links listed under one domain, such as school.discovery.com. True or false?

9. When I create my virtual index in AltaVista, putting phrases in quotation marks is meaningless. True or false?

10. When I create my virtual index in AltaVista I need to remove the _____ from the URL.
    a. http://
    b. www.
    c. Both http:// and www.
    d. None of the above.

11. Match the country on the left to the appropriate country code on the right.

United States	.ca
United Kingdom	.cn
South Africa	.za
Canada	.uk
India	.jp
Israel	.mx
Mexico	.es
Spain	.in
China	.us
Japan	.il

12. If I want to search for .k12 sites across the United States, the best command to use is the host: command. True or false?

13. If I wish to search through schools in the United States with the host: command, I must also include a state and the country code *.us*. True or false?

14. A search for .edu sites using the url: command will not only find .edu sites, it will also find sites that include the word *education* or *educator* in the URL.

Answer Key: 1. 1 c, 2 e, 3 a, 4 h, 5 d, 6 f, 7 b, 8 g; 2. False; 3. d; 4. b; 5. True; 6. c; 7. False; 8. True; 9. False; 10. c; 11. United States, .us, United Kingdom, .uk, South Africa, .za, Canada, .ca, India, .in, Israel, .il, Mexico, .mx, Spain, .es, China, .cn, Japan, .jp; 12. False; 13. True; 14. True

QUESTIONS FOR EXTENDED THOUGHT AND DISCUSSION

1. Do you think the doctor telling his patient not to go to the Internet for research was the best strategy for the patient?

2. How can you apply the concept of searching with an extension or country code in your curriculum or work?

3. Imagine a teacher who has conducted a search for *host:ac.jp +* *"world war II" + hiroshima*. The Japanese view of what happened in Hiroshima is very different than what is presented in American textbooks. Would you open your class to this kind of challenge to your own country's viewpoint?

4. Would you encourage your students to bring resources to class that they found on other teachers' Web sites?

Expanding the Boundaries

Blogs, RSS, Podcasts, and Wikis

This chapter is a joy to write. It is a celebration of the amazing work of pioneering educators who have been willing to expand the boundaries of learning for their students. While the words *blog, wiki,* and *podcast* are used to describe the enabling technologies, the real focus of this chapter is connecting students to an authentic audience and challenging them to create work that can have an impact around the world. Of course, to a student the word *blog* means free Web site and a potential connection to friends and the power of expression. Alternatively, in many schools, the word *blog* represents something that is automatically blocked via the Internet filter.

Of course, no one can argue that there is very questionable content on free blogging sites such as MySpace and Facebook, where students may expand their voices around the world. A small number of students have produced totally inappropriate and even vicious content. Blocking blogs in school is a natural first response against the potential deep harm this medium can create. However, now that blogging has gone mainstream (e.g., in presidential politics, corporate communications, higher education) it is time to revisit the upside of preparing students to understand the ethics and social responsibility that comes with all of this global power.

If we can all agree that students do not need our permission to have a blog when they leave the school house, then let's focus on the teachable moment. Our students need us to provide the excellent role models and the thoughtful ethics this medium demands. Blogs are not going away.

Indeed, essentially all of the major 2008 U.S. presidential candidates used blogs to connect with the next generation of voters. If we do not teach our students how this powerful media works, the worst case may not be student abuse. To paraphrase Marshall McLuhan, the real danger is that a majority of our students will lack the critical-thinking skills necessary to separate the message from the medium.

Chris's Story

During a workshop where I was exposed to blogging for the first time, I stood up and walked out of the room thinking, no way—I'm not doing it. A year later, I'm convinced blogging is now central to student motivation and the whole process of students taking more responsibility for the quality of their work. I have never had students who are so excited about writing. For the first time in my career, I have students who are submitting their writing to me without an assignment, just so they can have their work published for review by an authentic global audience.

While my class was reading *Mississippi Trial, 1955,* a novel by Chris Crowe, we were excited one particular morning to see a new comment on our class blog. It was from Mr. Crowe himself. He replied saying, "I'm especially pleased by your students' reaction to my characters; I tried to make the fictional people as complicated and interesting as people are in real life. The students' insight into the issues and characters are right on, and it's clear they're doing careful reading and thinking. I'm looking forward to talking to everyone in a week or two."

Perhaps what surprised me the most is that when the school year finished, I had students who continued to reflect on their writing during our summer vacation. It is very validating to me to have a student come back to school to share how they visited the class blog during their vacation to see if there were any comments from around the world.

Chris's middle school students are participating in what is probably the most powerful opportunity the Internet can provide—the ability to communicate within a global forum, build knowledge content as a community, and publish writing to an authentic audience. Think about how motivating it would be as a middle school student to have feedback on your writing from the real-life author of a book you are reading in class. Even better, as this entire blog project built momentum, Mr. Crowe ended up going to visit Chris's class and met her students face to face.

Not all bloggers are going to have the opportunity to meet with nationally acclaimed authors, but the ability to communicate with any-one around the world—experts in your community or peer-editors in Japan—is entirely possible.

BLOGGING

Blogging represents one of many tools that pioneering teachers are using to empower students to take more responsibility of managing their own work and adding value to the world. Thousands of teachers are using blogs as educational tools: they are relatively easy to create, you can cre-ate content in minutes, you can publish to a large audience or a targeted community, and you can invite almost anyone into a conversation. Even so, there are also some fierce critics who believe blogging has no true value in the classroom. Each has an important voice.

Here are some of the common concerns I've heard from other teach-ers about blogging:

- Blogs give too much freedom for students to express themselves.
- Teachers will never be able to control comments.
- Students and parents will have too much access to other students' published work.
- Students will feel too much pressure to improve as they see the work and comments of others.

Shifts of Control

Unlike word processing, using a smart board, or having students pre-sent a PowerPoint presentation to classmates behind closed doors, blog-ging shifts the concept of the control of information. Perceptions of time, space, and relationships are expanded. The audience moves from teacher and class to the world. Teachers are no longer the sole or even the primary arbitrator of student work. It is even possible that teachers do not have to work as hard to motivate traditionally failing students or to set much higher expectations for excelling students. Parents can now have access to the writing of an entire class, compared to only what their own child brings home written in their hand. Because of her blog, Chris has had requests from Turkey and the Caribbean for writing partnerships this year.

Building Knowledge

Enter *"pre cal"* into Google and in one of the top spots you will find http://pc40s.blogspot.com/. This is the class blog of Winnipeg math teacher and department head, Darren Kuropatwa. Darren is another pioneer who has engaged his students in producing a student guide to precalculus and calculus. Each day a different student is the official scribe of the class and is responsible for producing notes for publication of that day's discussion. Students are challenged to produce accurate notes with accompanying illustrations and examples by their classmates. At the end of this year, his classes will have produced a *Student's Guide to Understanding Calculus.* Before blogging we would expect hardworking students to be able to read the calculus textbook. Darren expects his students to write the "book"—i.e., blog.

Darren's students are published around the world in real time. In fact, a recent check using the link: command in AltaVista shows hundreds of Web sites linked to the class site, including conferences and commentaries by leading educationalists and other math teachers. (Go to AltaVista and type: *link:http://pc40s.blogspot.com* to generate today's list.)

Darren knows the power of students who understand that their work is being referenced by organizations around the world. His students are contributors to the world's "knowledge commons." Not only does he teach calculus, he teaches students that one of the responsibilities of global citizenship is publishing knowledge products to add value to the world.

Bump in the Night

As with all technologies there can be serious abuses. We must balance the few amazing stories of blogging with what can go very wrong. We have all heard the horror stories of what can happen when students pick up a free blog from Blogger, Facebook, MySpace, and many other free sites. Death threats to fellow classmates and inappropriate pictures by young teen girls who are looking for dates are horrible examples that are local to me.

The Pew Charitable Trust, a leading Internet in Society research organization, reports that a fifth of students in the United States already have their own blogs, and this number is growing. As with e-mail, instant messenger, and text messaging, the question is not about whether students will be blogging. Eventually, the majority of students probably will have a blog. The real issue is what is the professional response to blogging? Because of abuse on the public sites that are not controlled by teachers, some schools are blocking all access to any blogging sites. The blame is on the technology and there is no opportunity for pioneering teachers to provide adult role models. (As a point of information, with the right software, all comments to a class blog can be moderated by the teacher for complete judicial control.)

Using the medium to teach responsibility is a direction recommended by Anne Davis (http://anne.teachesme.com/) from Georgia State. Anne works in the College of Education in the Instructional

Technology Center. She writes, even when talking to second graders about blogging and about how to leave a comment, "I talked briefly about being ambassadors, of their class, their school, their state, country, and yes even the world. I spent time on the importance of learning how to use a tool well and being a good representative of responsible use of that tool. I'm planting blogging seeds so that when they are teenagers and want to 'write all,' maybe, just maybe, they'll ponder the possible results" (Davis, 2006).

We will need courageous leaders willing to explore the strengths and weaknesses of this medium. Our students will live in a world where they have access to increasingly more powerful communications tools. Who should teach them how to manage the power of these tools?

Role Models and Safety Issues

The amount of personal information many students post on their personal blogs is staggering. In many ways it's important for teachers to consider the use of blogs in the classroom if only to model appropriate behavior of this powerful communication tool and provide students with guidance and precaution about keeping themselves safe.

Keeping children safe on the Web is obviously a very serious issue. If you plan on creating a blog for classroom use, here are guidelines you should consider.

- Choose a blogging service that offers moderating features. To protect the integrity of your blog and ensure it garners no inappropriate comments, you will want to be able to read comments first before they are published.
- Instead of using student names, consider having students use pseudonyms or class numbers.
- When posting student writing, be careful about publishing materials that include personal information that will identify students to the outside world.
- If you have younger students (13 and younger) and wish to blog, you must be familiar with the Children's Online Privacy Protection Act (COPPA; Federal Trade Commission, 1998). See Coppa.org.
- Cyber bullying is a real threat. Do not expect students to create their own blogs for classroom use *unless* you have precautions in place to carefully monitor their content and the comments they receive. In other words, please do not set your students up to be targeted in any way, shape, or form.
- Check to see if your school requires a parental consent form before beginning.

School-based software blog packages can target most of these safety issues, as they control the user environment.

How Can You Blog?

The most effective uses of blogs in classrooms generally focus on the following. Consider creating blog posts for:

- Discussion topics for students—once you post a question, students can post feedback (it's possible to monitor feedback) and respond to your comments and other students' comments.
- Discussion topics for the community—anyone in the world can participate in your blog discussions. You may consider teaming up with another teacher in another city or solicit members of your community to join in; for example, ask an expert.
- Build community—post announcements, homework, and upcoming events—your blog can be an ongoing dialogue/bulletin board for you, students, and parents. (Research suggests that parental involvement is a huge indicator of a student's success in school.)
- Publish student work—you may publish student writing to showcase or for peer review. Consider teaming with members of the global community to help your students edit or assess their work.
- Create a forum for collaboration with other students—online projects with students around the world can develop through the use of blogs.
- Build a body of knowledge—for example, Darren's AP Calculus class will have a textbook and study guide complete by the end of the year. This will be a great resource for next year's students to access a year's worth of notes, or for graduates from that class to look back and find notes that might help them in college.

RSS

One of the amazing technologies that sit behind blogs and many other Web-based tools is RSS. Think of RSS as an automatic syndicating network. Anyone who subscribes to a blog's RSS feed will automatically receive new content produced on the blog without having to go back to the blog Web site. RSS enables anyone to become a worldwide publisher. Think of the ethics and social responsibility of this tool.

You may have noticed that many Web sites these days have an orange button or a link with the letters RSS or XML. RSS stands for *Real Simple Syndication* and is usually referred to as a *feed*. Harnessing the power of

RSS means that you can subscribe to a feed from other sites—be it Web logs, Web sites, photo galleries, podcasts, and so on. Remember when you learned to save a Web site address in your favorites? Feeds are much more powerful. Bookmarking a Web site requires you to go back to the site to see if there is any new information on the site. Subscribing to the RSS feed provides you with information as soon as the content hits the Web site. In a sense, feeds allow you to become your own editor in chief of managing information from around the world.

Bringing feeds into a central location is done with the help of a tool called an *aggregator.* Applying for an account is usually free, and once you have your account you can set it to collect and manage information directly for you from an infinite number of sources. For example, hundreds of traditional media outlets, such as the *New York Times, Newsweek,* and the *Wall Street Journal* now offer RSS feeds for their content. (RSS is still gaining popularity. Be aware, many sites do not yet have RSS feed technology.)

Instead of physically going out to find information from these sites, or a top academic journal in a certain field, you can subscribe to feeds that aggregate to a single site. Any new information about a topic is automatically collected in your aggregator. The research comes directly to you and you can generate mountains of quality information in your sleep—literally. Think of the implications for students and their ability to conduct research. If students can have information about a given topic delivered to them from ten separate trusted academic sources every day, the amount of information they amass will be incredible. I have a folder on my Bloglines aggregator that manages feeds about climate change from sources all over the world. What the BBC publishes about climate change can be quite different than the feeds from the *New York Times.* All of this content comes to me as soon as it is available.

What is fascinating to me is that I have met students who continue to subscribe to their feeds long after the assignment is due. RSS is an essential tool for lifelong learning.

RSS for Teachers

Aside from a personal selection of newspapers or journals you may want delivered to your personal aggregator door, educators might consider receiving feeds from their favorite blog authors or from other teachers. If you are a middle school English teacher and you like the work that Chris is doing on her blog, you might want to have any new assignments she posts on her site to come to you as well. If you are a math teacher, and your students might find the notes from Darren's classes in Winnipeg helpful to what you are doing in your class, you can sign up to receive each post.

If you are already oversaturated with volumes of information on the Web as it is, you may decide never to use this tool. However, just keep in mind that using the Internet is the number one research choice of our students. Knowing how to harness the power of RSS is an essential skill. If you want to give your students the edge in doing academic research—especially when they get to college—teach them this tool!

How It's Done

The best way to get started collecting or subscribing to feeds is to open an account at a free aggregator service, such as Bloglines (http://www.bloglines.com/).

To set up an account in Bloglines, begin by clicking on the registration link on the top right corner of the page. You will be taken to a form that asks for your e-mail address, your preferred password, and a few other easy pieces of information. Click on the register button and you will receive an e-mail asking you to confirm your account. Upon confirmation, you will be taken into your account, and you can begin adding your feeds. Before doing this, however, you need to do a bit of legwork—namely, find the sites from which you would like feeds to come.

For example, if you wanted to have feed coming into a Bloglines account from the *New York Times* (http://www.nytimes.com/), you need to find that code before adding it to your site. The *New York Times* has established specific RSS code for each of its newspaper sections and some writers, such as Thomas Friedman. At the bottom of the *New York Times* home page is a link:

Add New York Times RSS feeds **XML**

Clicking the link will take you to a page with a long list of the sections available for RSS feeds. By clicking any of these orange boxes, you will be taken to a page filled with RSS code (see below).

Pay no attention to the body of this page—you are only interested in the URL. You need this Web address to create a feed in your Bloglines account. Highlight and copy the address in the location bar.

Address [icon] http://www.nytimes.com/services/xml/rss/nyt/Education.xml

Note: Another option for selecting this feed is to put your cursor over the RSS icon of the feed you are choosing to subscribe to and right clicking on that icon. You will be prompted to copy the link location.

With the URL in tow, go back to your Bloglines account and add the RSS to your feeds (click Add, paste the URL into the field provided, and click Subscribe). Now the feed has been added to your account. Whenever there is new content, you can view it in your Bloglines account. It's your very own Web subscription service.

Tips for RSS

Harnessing the power of RSS feeds can be a powerful method of research for both you and your students. Here are some ideas:

- If students are researching a particular unit of study, you can create RSS feeds from online journals or publications particular to that subject.
- Teachers can create feeds from their favorite bloggers—or tap into resources from other teacher blogs. The best place to find teacher blogs is in the search engine Technorati (http://www .technorati.com/).
- Daily headlines from around the world can appear on your site.
- If your students have their own community or blog sites, you can obtain feeds from them.
- RSS also allows you to subscribe to podcasts.

PODCASTS

Mr. Blake's Story

Why is a science teacher interested in using podcasting in a science classroom? This requires us to review how knowledge and understanding is impacted by classroom instruction. Podcasting allows students time to explore areas of curiosity.

From an instructional point of view, my kids could be using our dusty cassette recorders to record podcasts, which might not necessarily be a bad idea. I overheard one of my best students tell his classmate that he was going to go to Wal-Mart when he went home to buy a microphone to use on his mom's computer to record his own podcasts. Well, that spoke volumes. He is now self-motivated to learn and explore new avenues of expression. Through experiencing podcasting in our classroom, he is now excited about the potential of his knowledge. To me, in my humble opinion, this is what education is really all about. He is now the expert. Before we started podcasting, this student had never experienced success in the classroom. However, he is now a leader. It's like magic. The consistent positive feedback from his peers has really boosted his confidence and is what has produced the changes I have witnessed.

This idea of empowering students to create their own voice in what they are thinking and ultimately learning goes along with helping them become lifelong learners. If they are auditory learners, the spoken word is invaluable to them. Podcasting helps them find that voice and no matter where they end up in life, the ability to communicate is going to be a tremendous skill for them to have.

A podcast is an audio or video file, which can be downloaded to a computer, iPod, MP3 player, or any number of handheld devices. Anyone can subscribe to a podcast once the right software has been downloaded onto your machine (software downloads are available for free). Podcasts are available by visiting a podcaster's Web site for a direct download, or by subscribing to a podcast's feed through RSS, whereby new podcasts are automatically delivered to you.

Creating podcasts in the classroom is a creative way to reach learners and tap into a technology many young people already enjoy outside of class. The ability to record conversations, lessons, and projects gives students the opportunity to publish their work to an authentic audience. Multimedia projects can be published online to worldwide viewers. Parents can see video or hear a recording of their child's latest band concert, or see a portfolio of artwork or a skit in a foreign language class. Parents can also create an RSS feed from their child's school blog so that anything that any podcast posted to the blog comes directly home to them—or wherever they may be.

An inspiring example of a teacher who has expanded the boundaries and motivation level of his classroom is Bob Sprankle of Wells, Maine.

Bob spent time guiding his third and fourth grade students through an introduction to podcasting. He gave student teams jobs as writers, producers, and technicians. Over time, his students took control of the class podcast and amazing things began happening. Time was spent during snack periods organizing, recording, and publishing podcasts that could be subscribed to anywhere in the world. Over time, their skills grew and their podcasts gained a broader audience. After many podcasts, including one with a local senator, these students were invited to present to teachers at the University of Southern Maine for the Maine Learning Technology Initiative.

Universities are also providing podcasts that allow anyone who has the desire, to learn from their instructors. UC Berkeley and MIT are just two examples of universities providing lectures online for free. This service offers students who attend these universities an opportunity to download lectures for review as needed, but that's not all. These podcasts are available to anyone. We can all subscribe to these courses and learn from top researchers. Sorry, you don't get the degree at the end.

To start exploring the vast number of podcasts available, I encourage you to download iTunes from Apple (http://www.apple.com/iTunes/). This program, available for the Macintosh and PC, is currently the easiest and most full-featured way to find, subscribe to, and listen to podcasts. Once you have downloaded and installed iTunes, podcasts are only moments away.

To begin searching for educational podcasts within iTunes, click on the link to the Music Store in the left column. Then, within that same column, you will see another link to Podcasts. Scroll down to the bottom of the page until you see a Categories list. Select *Education.* Select *K–12* as a subcategory. You will see a long alphabetical list of podcasts. You can click on any one to listen to it. It may take a moment or two for it to start.

iTunes stores a list of the podcasts, but not the files themselves. The podcast is brought to you from the Web to iTunes, to your player, using RSS. If you click on a title of any podcast, you will hear a sampling from the podcast. To hear the entire podcast click the Subscribe button. (You can always delete it later.)

Now, if you want to move from subscribing podcasts to recording your own, you will want to download some audio recording software. You might consider Audacity (http://audacity.sourceforge.net/), which is available for both Mac and PC. My strong recommendation is to have two students learn how to use the program (homework) and then have them come back to class to teach you the basics.

WIKIS

Natalie's Story

Each year, my third grade class visits the historic Pitot House, an 18th-century Creole colonial plantation located in New Orleans, Louisiana. We do a great deal to prepare for this trip. Weeks in advance, each of my students is assigned a character that at one time was affiliated with the home in some way. From there, the students do a good bit of research on the plantation, as well as their individual characters. Finally, during the culminating visit to the plantation, the whole class presents biographies of their characters (in full dress) at the plantation home for numerous visitors.

I have recently become very excited with what wikis have to offer, and this year, I decided to take a look at Wikipedia to see if there was a listing for the Pitot House. There wasn't. Seeing this as a great opportunity for my students to further develop what they have already learned, as well as to actually write a piece of history, we worked as a class to develop our own Wikipedia article.

The students were thrilled to see their work online; especially as they learned that their work was going to be seen by the whole world. Knowing this outcome, they were all much more engaged in the writing and editing of the article.

A few days later, we were so excited to see that a complete stranger had gotten onto our article and added a picture of the house as well as a new link branching off to more information. In the future, my classes will be able to take what past classes have written and really enhance the work further.

If you have never run across a wiki before, it is nothing more than a Web-based tool that allows people to work together on a single piece of writing or a body of work. This work might be a group research paper; an Acceptable Use Policy created for your school by faculty, students, and parents; or even an article within an encyclopedia. Yes, even the traditional encyclopedia has become an interactive, fluid publication through the efforts of people all over the world who take part in the Wikipedia project.

Say That Again, an Encyclopedia That Anyone Can Edit?

Wikipedia offers all knowledge consumers and producers the opportunity to take part in building the world's largest interactive knowledge base. All you have to do is visit http://www.wikipedia.org/ and search for an article that is of interest to you. If you have some important information to add to the topic, you can simply add it. If you see an error in the article, you can fix it. It's that simple! Just click the edit button within each article and add your information. When you click the save button, your information becomes a part of a community of hundreds of thousands of other Wikipedians. The concept of Wikipedia is that the knowledge of the masses and constant editing of the masses will produce a knowledge product that is powerful.

Quality Control

If the concept of wikis is fairly new to you, you may be thinking, "Wait a minute, if anyone can contribute to a body of knowledge, such as an article about Shakespeare, how do I know the information listed here is correct?"

You're right to think that. Somebody with absolutely no expertise on a subject can write or edit an article on any subject. Wikipedia has had some bad press concerning some of the inaccuracies contained within their articles, but the Wikipedia community does a really great job of policing their knowledge community. When an entry (edit or addition) is made to a wiki page, community members are constantly working together to check the validity of the entry. But be forewarned that this site is "live" so validation will not necessarily be instantaneous.

Just as you would not allow students to research only within one book, you also should not allow them to research from only one Web site. Students should be finding information and cross-referencing what they find with other online and print resources. Additionally, they should be looking to and citing the primary sources from which the information within each article is coming. Wikipedia, or any source, is only one small piece of a larger picture.

If you really want to see the power of what Wikipedia has to offer, you should take a moment to check out some of the cited materials at the end of most entries. For example, go to Wikipedia, and search for *"Abraham Lincoln"* or something simple like *frogs.* Let's assume there are some mistakes in both articles. Let's push that idea aside for a moment and scroll down to the bottom of each entry. Just look at all of the valuable, cited resources listed here. I'm sure you'll agree that finding all of these sources without the help of Wikipedia would take quite a while.

Looking Beyond Wikipedia

While Wikipedia is the most well-known wiki out there, it is not all that wikis can offer to a classroom teacher who is working toward building community between his or her classroom and others around the world. Wiki software is available that will allow teachers and students to work collaboratively in a protected environment. This software, including PBwiki (http://www.pbwiki.com/) and Wikispaces (http://www.wiki spaces.com/) is easy to setup, easy to use, and easy to protect.

To get a good idea of how wikis can be used in this way, I encourage you to look at the wiki project organized by John Bidder. In the wiki he manages (http://www.wikiville.org.uk/), he has opened up a space where students from all over the world can come together and tell the stories of their lives from wherever it is that they are located. As this project grows, it will be a fantastic source of first-hand accounts of day-to-day life. It's an outstanding, growing project. Additionally, Seth Bowers has created a wiki (http://dps109.wikispaces.com/Skype/) and he has shared information on a project designed by a teacher in the school where he works. In this project, students are learning first hand the effects globalization will have on them in the future. You will notice in the top right corner of his wiki page that this wiki is protected. Only those with a password can contribute to this one.

CONCLUSION

Blogs, RSS feeds, podcasts, and wikis are just some of the examples of powerful tools now available for teachers and students. Over time these tools will change, but the ability to expand our boundaries to a global community and open up new methods of authentic assessment is here to stay. These are technologies our young people are currently using and many will be expected to use once they enter the workplace. Providing them with guidance and positive role models about how to harness their power is essential. If we abdicate our responsibility to provide role models, our worst fears about the abuse of these technologies will come true.

RESOURCES

Anne Davis (http://anne.teachesme.com/)

Bloglines (http://www.bloglines.com/)

COPPA (http://www.coppa.org/)

Darren Kuropatwa's Pre-Calculus Blog (http://pc40s.blogspot.com/)

John Bidder's wiki (Wikiville) (http://www.wikiville.org.uk/)

New York Times (http://www.nytimes.com/)

PBwiki (http://www.pbwiki.com/)

Seth Bowers' wiki (DPS 109) (http://dps109.wikispaces.com/Skype/)

Technorati (http://www.technorati.com/)

Wikipedia (http://www.wikipedia.org/)

Wikispaces (http://www.wikispaces.com/)

ASSESSMENT

1. It's a good idea for teachers to moderate comments to their blogs to ensure inappropriate comments are not published on their site. True or false?

2. Which of the following is a suggested safety precaution for teachers using blogs in the classroom?
   a. Students should post their first and last names when contributing to the blog.
   b. Teachers should restrict parent access to their site.
   c. Students should not publish materials that include information that will identify them to the outside world.
   d. Teachers should monitor all feeds to their site.

3. How does RSS actually work?
   a. It allows you to subscribe to feeds from other sites through an aggregator. Once that is in place, any new content from those sites is delivered right to you.
   b. It puts an aggregator into an RSS feed and sends you e-mail.
   c. It brings you content from Web sites. You do that by cutting and pasting the entire body of XML into an aggregator.

4. A podcast is audio or video content that can be downloaded to an MP3 player or an iPod. True or false?

5. The strength of wikis is that they allow for group collaboration and knowledge building. True or false?

6. Wikipedia can be a valuable part of the research process if:
   a. Students cross-reference the information they find with other sources.
   b. Students use the vast array of cited documents at the end of each Wikipedia article.
   c. Both a and b.
   d. Wikipedia should never be used as a part of the research process.

Answer Key: 1. True; 2. c; 3. a; 4. True; 5. True; 6. c

QUESTIONS FOR FURTHER
THOUGHT AND DISCUSSION

1. Have educators lost control of the information that their students can access?

2. What responsibilities do schools have about teaching students the ethics about blogging?

3. What are your thoughts on the concept that publishing student work for a global audience can lead to more effort and reflective review by the student?

4. Similar to the third grade students in Natalie's New Orleans classroom, what content can your students create that will add value to the world?

5. Under what conditions can Wikipedia be a source of information for your students?

Strategies and Evaluation

Putting It All Together

Art's Story

I first became aware of the need to teach critical thinking in 1996 when teaching Internet Basics. Students had to pick a social issue and create a Web site around it. One pair had posed the question, "Are professional athletes paid too much?"

They called me over one day, showed me a Web site, and asked if I had seen it before. (It was called *The College Entrance Exam for Football Players,* a parody site.) I said yes and began to walk away. At that point one of them made a comment that stopped me in my tracks. He said, "It's sooooo easy!"

I turned around and quietly said, "Hey guys, *The College Entrance Exam for Football Players* is not a real exam. On the real exam they don't ask questions like, "How many feet in 0.0 meters?"

I didn't know whether to laugh or cry. This is just one of many teachable moments on the topic of Web literacy.

Helping students develop research and critical-thinking skills on the Web can be a daunting task. So much information is available to them and so many helpful tools, that sometimes knowing how to begin can be overwhelming for both students and teachers.

This chapter serves as a synthesis of some of the steps and resources necessary to validate Web site information. These steps, along with the included guiding questions, will help you teach REAL search strategies to your students.

GET REAL

As explored in Chapters 3 and 4, REAL outlines four steps in validating Web site information:

R = Read the URL

E = Examine the content

A = Ask about the author and publisher

L = Look at the links

R = Read the URL

Do you recognize the domain name?

What is the extension in the domain name?

Are you on a personal page?

E = Examine the Content

Is the information on the site helpful?

Does the site have more resources and links? Do the links work?

Is the site up to date? Can you tell when it was last updated?

Is the information correct?

Are the facts different from information you have found elsewhere?

A = Ask About the Author and Owner

Is the author's name on the site?

Is there a contact person or e-mail address?

Is there any information about the author?

Does the author know the topic well? Is he or she an expert?

L = Look at the Links

Forward Links:

What are the URLs of the forward links?

Do the domain names change?

Is the information biased?

Back Links:

Who is linked to the Web site?

Why they are linked?

What do other sites say about the information on the site?

REAL RESOURCES

Here is a list of online and print resources students can access to practice their validating and critical-thinking skills.

Validating Tools

Wayback Machine (http://www.archive.org/). Use this site to see the history of a Web site.

easyWhois (http://www.easywhois.com/). Use this site to find out who owns a Web site.

AltaVista (http://www.altavista.com/). Use the link: command in AltaVista to find the external links from any site.

Sites for Students to Validate

A Short Introduction to the Study of Holocaust Revisionism (http://pubweb.northwestern.edu/~abutz/di/intro.html; *now can be found by entering the above URL into the Wayback Machine at Archive.org.*). This site is appropriate for use in middle or high school. It is written by an engineering professor at Northwestern University and contains racist and offensive material. It presents a version of the truth and is a clear example of why students need to think critically about information on the Internet.

All about Explorers (http://www.allaboutexplorers.com/). This is a great site for all ages. Check out the exercises.

California Velcro Crop under Challenge (http://home.inreach.com/ kumbach/velcro.html). Use this fun site to help students separate fact from fiction on the Web.

Dihydrogen Monoxide (http://www.dhmo.org/). Who knew water could be so hazardous? This is a good site to use with middle school students. Have students click through the forward links on the site. Have them check to see if the Web site references any other authors.

Dog Island Free Forever (http://www.thedogisland.com/). A puppy dog paradise. This is a great site for all ages.

Feline Reactions to Bearded Men (http://improbable.com/airchives/ classical/cat/cat.html). This is a fun site to use when teaching students how to validate Web resources. Science teachers take note! This site pokes fun at the scientific method.

Martin Luther King (http://www.martinlutherking.org/). The site at this seemingly innocent Web address calls for the abolition of Martin Luther King Day and promotes white pride. This content is inappropriate for all students. Contains racist and offensive material.

The Pacific Northwest Tree Octopus (http://zapatopi.net/treeoctopus/). This is a great site to use with all ages. Have students click through the links and read the Web addresses carefully.

Victorian Robots (http://www.bigredhair.com/robots/index.html). This is a great site to use with all ages. It has even stumped historians. Have students truncate the Web address so they are just left with the domain name. This will give them some insight into the validity of this site.

Common Extensions

Here is a list of common extensions.

.edu	Higher education (most U.S. colleges)
.k12	U.S. school site (not all U.S. schools use this)
.sch	Schools in the United Kingdom (not all U.K. schools use this)
.ac	Academic institution (usually outside of the United States)
.com	Commercial
.org	Any organization
.gov	Government agency

.net   Network

.mil   U.S. military

Country Codes

Here are some examples of country codes.

.at	Austria	.ie	Ireland
.au	Australia	.in	India
.ca	Canada	.iq	Iraq
.ch	Switzerland	.it	Italy
.cn	China	.jp	Japan
.de	Germany	.nz	New Zealand
.es	Spain	.pk	Pakistan
.et	Ethiopia	.uk	United Kingdom
.fr	France	.us	United States
.gr	Greece	.za	South Africa

E = EXAMINE THE CONTENT WORKSHEET

For each site you visit, answer these questions.

Web site _____

Is the information on the site helpful? Yes/No

Does the site have more resources and links? Do the links work? Yes/No

Is the site up to date? Can I tell when it was last updated? Yes/No

Is the information correct? Yes/No

Are the facts different from information I have found elsewhere? Yes/No

Web site _____

Is the information on the site helpful? Yes/No

Does the site have more resources and links? Do the links work? Yes/No

Is the site up to date? Can I tell when it was last updated? Yes/No

Is the information correct? Yes/No

Are the facts different from information I have found elsewhere? Yes/No

Web site _____

Is the information on the site helpful? Yes/No

Does the site have more resources and links? Do the links work? Yes/No

Is the site up to date? Can I tell when it was last updated? Yes/No

Is the information correct? Yes/No

Are the facts different from information I have found elsewhere? Yes/No

TIPS FOR SEARCHING WITH THE LINK: COMMAND

The link: command allows you to create a list of external links. It is an excellent validating tool if you are unsure about the quality of information on a Web site.

How Do I Start?

1. Go to AltaVista, and in the search box, type *link:*.

2. Leaving no space after the colon, type the address of the Web site you are researching. For example, to find the back links to the site Feline Reactions to Bearded Men, type the following in the search box: *link:http://www.improbable.com/airchives/classical/cat/cat.html.*

3. Click the Find button and you will find an assortment of sites.

0 Results?

If you are researching a URL and produce no results, try truncating the URL. To truncate, delete one folder at a time, moving from right to left. Each time delete to the previous slash.

Removing */airchives/classical/cat/cat.html* from the Feline Reaction to Bearded Men search mentioned above will provide a longer list of results.

References

Crowe, C. (2002). *Mississippi trial, 1955.* New York: Penguin.

Davis, A. (2006, January 19). Can we use our own email? *EduBlog Insights.* Retrieved September 11, 2007, from http://anne.teachesme.com/2006/01/19

Federal Trade Commission. (1998). *Children's online privacy protection act of 1998.* Retrieved September 11, 2007, from http://www.ftc.gov/ogc/coppa1.htm

Lenhart, A., & Madden, M. (2005). Teen content creators and consumers. *Pew Internet & American Life Project.* Retrieved September 11, 2007, from http://www.pewinternet.org/PPF/r/166/report_display.asp

Tan, A. (2003). *The opposite of fate.* New York: Penguin.

Index

CORWIN PRESS

The Corwin Presslogo—a raven striding across an open book—represents the union of courage and learning. Corwin Press is committed to improving education for all learners by publishing books and other professional development resources for those serving the field of PreK–12 education. By providing practical, hands-on materials, Corwin Press continues to carry out the promise of its motto: **"Helping Educators Do Their Work Better."**